# Bridging The Gap

Understanding The Transition After High School
& Structuring Your Ministry So That Your
Students Are Prepared

# Bridging The Gap

Understanding The Transition After High School
& Structuring Your Ministry So That Your
Students Are Prepared

Tommy McGregor

# Contents

Introduction - My Story                        9

Chapter 1 - The Great Gap                      15

Chapter 2 - The Gap Effects                    26

Chapter 3 - Adolescents in Transition          40

Chapter 4 - Transitional Discipleship          54

Chapter 5 - The Ownership Wheel                68

Chapter 6 - The Senior Year Initiative         85

Chapter 7 - The Follow-up Plan                 95

Chapter 8 - Transition Central                 105

Vision & Outline Plan                          115

About The Author                               124

Links & QR Codes                               125

To my mentors, in life & ministry,
who discipled and taught me the value of ownership.

## Introduction - My Story

I was sitting in a storage closet-turned youth ministry office, feeling the weight of the world on my shoulders. I was 22 years old and in my first official ministry position as the youth pastor of a small church not far from the seminary I was attending. On my mind that afternoon was a class of 12th graders, eagerly anticipating graduation from high school and the freedoms that awaited them on the other side. Thinking back on my own transition from high school to college, tears began to fall to my desk as I prayed, "Lord, what do I do?" Unsure of the process, I knew that these teenage friends would soon be heading in the direction towards what had been the hardest spiritual struggle of my life. I didn't want them to make some of the same mistakes that I had made when I was in their shoes. I wanted them to be prepared for the challenges and freedoms of life after high school.

When I was in high school, I was like the poster child for a teenage Christian youth group kid. I grew up in a healthy Christian family and was active in a church that taught about following Jesus. I was the one who invited friends to weekly outreach events and encouraged my peers in their faith. I led Bible studies for those younger than me and was even voted the president of my youth group, which still to this day I am not sure what that meant. I was the captain on the church league basketball team and received a plaque from my church, just before graduation, that read: "Tommy McGregor, 1990 Most Outstanding Senior." I was that guy, and I played the role well. Jesus said in Matthew 5 that we are called to be the light of the world, and we are not to cover our light but rather let it shine brightly for others to see. I was a bonfire of a light in high school, attracting my friends to gather around, make s'mores, and sing Kumbaya, all in the name of Jesus.

I remember getting ready to go to college and thinking that I would just continue to do what I had done in high school, in regards to my faith. I had gotten the most outstanding senior award, for goodness sake. If anyone was prepared for this challenge, it had to be be me. Looking back now, my life in high school was like rafting down the rapid white waters of a river. I didn't have to paddle very much, just hang on and enjoy the ride. Living out my faith was easy when I was in high school because it had yet to be challenged.

I spent the first three years of college searching for who I was. I had been jolted from a life of confidence in high school to one of insecurity in college. I had community, just not a healthy one. I made decisions, just not wise ones. I formed an identity, just not one that reflected a city on a hill. Just after taking my final exam to end my junior year in college, I was packing up my dorm room to go home for the summer. I remember loading up a couple bags of clothes, some boxes of books, and a few hundred CD's (that's how we rolled in the early 90's). As I unloaded my bookshelf with textbooks and such, I reached for the next book and grabbed my old Bible. This was the same Bible that I had taught a middle school Bible study from. These were the same pages that I had read in my own weekly small group and included all the underlines, notes, and inserts from years of growth prior to college. I paused as I felt the worn leather on the binding of this sacred book for the first time in a while. That moment brought me back emotionally to a place of direction, dedication and devotion to Jesus and a desire to follow Him and His Word. I took a break from packing to reminisce on the contrast of my life from then to now. I had not gone wild and crazy in college by most accounts, but I had certainly forgotten to keep my relationship with Jesus as the foundation on which I thought I had stood so firmly on in high school. I remember thinking that I liked the guy I was then, more than the one I had become. Three years had passed since my high school graduation, but I felt like I had just uncovered my light for the first time since that moment.

*The struggles that a teenager faces during this transition is not a college cultural problem, but rather a discipleship issue.*

Fast forward a year and a half of growth and maturity in my relationship with Jesus, I am back at my desk in the converted youth pastor office, with tears still coming down. I loved the kids in my first senior class, and I longed to help them understand what was just ahead and how to overcome their impending challenges. I pulled them all aside that week after our Wednesday night worship event and said that we were going to start meeting together to talk about their transition to college. I was excited and, since there is never a subject that a high school senior is more willing to talk about than college, they were excited, too. I can't remember what I taught them, but I do recall telling my story and answering lots of questions. The following year I started even sooner with the next senior class, and for the following two decades of full-time youth ministry, I focused extra attention on the senior class and their spiritual transition from high school to college. In 2006, I wrote a book called *Lost in Transition: Becoming Spiritually Prepared for College,* which is now in its 3rd edition. The book teaches college-bound students what it means to take ownership of their faith in that new setting. In 2010, I started an organization called TheTransMission, which is a ministry that trains leaders, equips parents, and prepares students for the transition to life after high school. Each day I am reminded of the grace that I was given as God redeemed my past to prepare me for a future calling.

So, the question that I have asked myself a million times in ministry, and one you have probably asked yourself as well, is *"How does a Christian teenager, with visible growth in his faith, struggle to the point of declining in maturity once he leaves home after graduation?"* If you have been in student ministry for any amount of time, you have noticed that each year kids go from confidence and a growing faith to insecurity and uncertainty, often in the time frame of one year after graduation. For some, it is a sliding slope that started a few years before graduation and only got steeper as time went on. For others, it is a clear Dr Jekyll and Mr Hyde scenario where everyone is left wondering what happened. For me, I have seen thousands struggle, just like I did, as they leave the nest of home and church and enter into the real world of college, the military, or the work force.

In the pages of this book, I hope to do two main things. First, I want to help you understand why this transition after high school is so difficult for Christian teenagers. Secondly, I hope to give you some insights for how to best prepare your students before they graduate, leave your ministry, and venture out into the world. My hope is that after you finish this book, you will have a better understanding of how to move forward with a transition-focused youth ministry as you structure your ministry so that you are fully preparing your students for the challenges ahead. I believe, as I will introduce in chapter four, that this is your number one priority in your ministry to teenagers.

I have been teaching the content of this book as a live workshop for over ten years. Hundreds of student ministry leaders have learned what you are about to learn and implemented this strategy in order to structure their ministry so that they are effectively preparing students for this transition. I hope the same for you as you work your way through this material. I purposely wrote this book without a lot of fluff so that you could get the content and finish it quickly. I also left you plenty of room on each page to take notes and write out ideas that come as you read.

It is important for you to understand that this book is a part of a bigger family of resources that will help you determine how to best prepare your students for this transition and then provide the student and parents with training to reach those goals. In the back of this book you will find a Transition Vision & Outline plan, as well as links to other information and useful tools. This will help you process the content presented in this book. Also, in the back pages, you will see a catalog of transitional discipleship books for young parents, high school seniors, parents of seniors, and college freshman. These resources can provide you with a full and effective transition curriculum that will benefit the families in your church, from children to college students.

## Chapter One - The Great Gap

It was the summer of 1997, and I was in my third year of full-time student ministry when I did something that no completely sane person called to loving kids in ministry should ever do: I took a group of high school students on a six day, 40-mile backpacking trip in the Rocky Mountains. At the time I was in my mid 20's and therefore either too confident or just naive enough to think that this would be a breeze. We dreamed of the experience as we drove from Texas to Colorado, and as the Rockies began to come into view, our excitement grew as high as the snow peaks. The night before the adventure, we celebrated our "Last Supper," knowing that our next week's meals would come from the sparse supplies that we would carry. The next morning, I remember putting on a semi-heavy pack on my back and plunging out into the wilderness for a journey yet to be understood in my mind as to its difficultly. The first few hours were easy, as they often are, walking on flat earth at the trailhead of an experience. Then came day two. The next morning we were all walking and having a great time together until the trail we were following literally ended at a cliff, not to be continued for 30 feet on the other side of a great gap. To make matters worse, between the bookending dirt trails was the white water of the Rio Grande River about 50 feet below.  Under these circumstances, I knew we had three options. One, we could go back, writing it off as "Oh well, sorry kids, but we tried!" kind of experience. Or, we could repel down the 50 foot rock wall, cross the river, and climb back up, which I was beginning to think was the reason we all had to sign a stack of waivers before setting off. Then, I guess, technically, we could go over it but I couldn't imagine that as a realistic option since none of us were named Clark Kent or Bruce Wayne. But luckily for us, our trail guides had gone ahead and constructed a complex roping system where you connected yourself to one part of the rope and pull yourself across with the other (opting for door number three). So, being the servant leader that I was, I chose to be the last to go so that I could "help" everyone else across and maybe test out the durability of the contraption in the meantime.

One by one, we sent each person across as our guides pulled from the other side. It took a couple of hours and ended up being safer, and far more fun, than any other alternative. It was a scary thing to see my high school friends suspended over rushing white water by a cord and a carabiniere, but we all made it without fail. Once I got across, we were ready to journey on together, up the mountain, following our experienced guides. That trip changed a lot of lives that week, mine included.

# The Great Gap of Student Discipleship

When I think about the transition that teenagers make after high school, I am reminded about the trail on my Colorado backpacking trip. For many during the high school years, the journey is straight and smooth and maybe somewhat easy. They are living at home, involved in your ministry, and life is simplified and carefree. Then, after graduation, they reach a gap in the trail that most did not see coming. They may or may not be focused enough to see the other side; and therefore, so many often opt to climb down and swim across. This detour can produce doubts and fears that are hard to recover from. This is the reason I refer to the transition after high school as the great gap of teenage discipleship.

As the guide on their spiritual journey through high school, your students need you to go ahead of them and construct a roping system to help them get across the great gap. This is new territory for them, and you need to help them realize that they shouldn't go back and they can not climb down. You will need to do this in three ways.

First, you must understand the need. Depending on where you look, there is a statistical range for how many Christian students struggle in their faith while attempting to cross this great gap. I can honestly tell you that it is somewhere between 60[1]-70[2]%. Do me a favor and try to erase the fact that you have heard this before. Attempt to re-read this sentence with a renewed perspective: Out of every one hundred teenagers who have professed Christ as Savor and grown up in a church, between sixty and seventy-five will drift away from growing and maturing in Christ after they graduate and leave home.

Obviously, some teenagers struggle more than others and many come back to their faith eventually, but the important thing is that the majority face a spiritual challenge that they are clearly not prepared for. And that is the key... they are not prepared.

According to the Fuller Youth Institute, only one in every seven high school seniors report feeling prepared to handle the challenges of college life.[3] This is not to say that they aren't prepared academically for college. Most high schools do a good job of helping students who are able to move forward to higher education. Many are not ill-prepared socially, and they certainly feel like they are ready to leave. Rather, these teenagers are not prepared to live on their own in their faith, while making wise decisions and continuing to grow and mature, like they did in high school.

Think of it this way. A typical Christian teenager has up to four major spiritual influences. Can you guess what those are? (I hope so, because you are

---

[1] "Most Twentysomethings Put Christianity on the Shelf Following Spiritually Active Teen Years", Barna, 2006

[2] "Reasons 18- to 22-Year-Olds Drop Out of Church", Lifeway, 2007

[3] "What Makes Faith Stick During College?" Fuller Youth Institute, 2011

most likely one of them.) Those four influences are: family, friends, church, and mentors. These influences have helped the teen grow and mature, from childhood until graduation. If a teenager grew up in a Christian home, was involved in a church, had Christ-centered friendships, and learned from mentors like you and others, then he or she is much like I was at that age. If you remember my story from the Introduction of this book, I grew up in an ideal Christian environment. I was a leader, I knew who I was, and I had even felt called to full-time ministry by my junior year in high school. I had all of those influences fully active in discipling me to follow Jesus. So, it's not that these students aren't mature or somehow have been going through the motions and playing the Christian role. Their faith is authentic. The problem is that these students do not know how to grow in their faith without those four influences. I know that was the case in my life as a teenager. I had those four influences intact, therefore I knew where to go for fellowship, discipleship, advice, and unconditional love. I had never made an important decision without seeking advice from those influences. Many of your students are the same way. They have never lived without these influences guiding them (& often holding their hand). Furthermore, they have never had to replace those influences in a new environment. They have never had to start over on the ground floor of developing community, as many teenagers have developed friendships over a span of years. They have probably not ever had to find a new church on their own, as many teenagers go to the same church their parents attend or they follow a close friend to church. When it comes to developing a mentoring relationship, mentors often seek out teenagers just as you have developed deeper relationships with your students. Also, they will not know how to seek out a mentor, much less that they even need to. As we know, adults (even college students) must often seek out mentoring relationships which can be difficult if the individual has never done that before. Lastly, even though a recent high school graduate feels ready to move away and live on his/her own, this will be the first time to have a long distance relationship with his/her family, and many students struggle to make that adjustment.

Let me add that this is also a hard transition for students who do not go off to college and possibly stay at home for the year after high school. For those students, some of the transitional differences are even greater. For these students, they are still at home and possibly at the same church, but everyone else is gone. They are no longer in the youth group (per se) and are now an adult living under the same roof as they did as a child. Mentally and developmentally, these college-aged students have moved up to adulthood, yet everything in their environment is just as it was in high school.

## This Is A Discipleship Issue

So, back to our original question of how a maturing Christian teenager can go from confidence to insecurity in a matter of months, it becomes easier to understand when one thinks of it in terms of the environmental changes that take place after graduation.

The struggles that a teenager faces during this transition is not a college cultural problem, but rather a discipleship issue. It is true that many older teens wander through this next stage of life as they get caught up in a worldly lifestyle, but that goes back to the point that they are not prepared to stand firmly in their faith in that new setting. Once we begin to understand the need to bridge this gap, we must determine the solution. Deep in my imagination, I can picture our guides from the backpacking trip looking at the gap in the trail and trying to determine the solution. The need was to get our group across to the other side, but how? Building stairs was out of the question and a helicopter was probably out of the budget, so they determined the method that would best reach the goal. Therefore, before we can go any further into this conversation, we must determine the process of reaching our goal of preparing them for this journey.

*I firmly believe that equipping a student with faith ownership before graduation is the only way to ensure that they make a healthy transition to life after high school.*

Since holding their hand and becoming a helicopter-mentor for the next 4+ years is out of the question (not to mention, spiritually irresponsible), the only real solution is to equip your students with faith ownership. Now, faith ownership is a term you are probably familiar with, but I want to make sure you understand the depth of what is necessary.

Think about the responsibility that comes with ownership. When describing this point to high school seniors in my book, *Lost in Transition*, I use the illustration of driving the old family car when I was a teenager as compared to today as I drive a vehicle that I picked out and paid for. The difference is ownership, and with ownership comes a commitment to protect, nurture, and grow. When I was a teenager, I was given a car that my Mom had driven for eight years. After the newness of driving wore off, I stopped taking care of the car and trashed it, inside and out. Now, I take good care of my vehicle because I have a sense of ownership over it. The same is true with our faith in Christ. We often hear the term "a borrowed faith" when describing a teenager without ownership. He comes to church because he is made to and is not proactive in maturing spiritually without hand-holding accountability. This is the most obvious example of a lack of ownership. The other side to this coin is the active teenager in your ministry that has enough ownership to grow in her own faith in high school. She is a leader and an example of a maturing Christian teenager. She is mature enough to continue growing in the environment of high school, but this student needs to be taught what I call Ownership 2.0, which is how to continue to grow and mature without the four influences that I described earlier in this chapter. We will go into more detail about how to best prepare each type of student in chapter four of this book.

The Bible has a lot to say about faith ownership. In 1 Corinthians 13:11, Paul writes: "When I was a child, I spoke like a child, I thought like a child, I reasoned like a child. When I became a man, I gave up childish ways."

As the writer of Hebrews puts it, "Let us leave the elementary doctrine of Christ and go on to maturity" (6:1). As a teenager gets older, we need to help them grow in maturity as well so that they develop ownership in their faith.

The first step to faith ownership is developing a sense of understanding. I have never been good at math and would always memorize the steps to solve an equation long enough to pass the test. That is often how believers approach their faith; they hear a Bible story or learn a verse long enough to know it for a Bible study but then forget it when it comes to applying it to life. Someone with ownership is mature enough to hear God's Word, understand how the passage is useful for living, and put in the effort to become a doer of God's Word (James 1:22).

Jesus spoke on this when he told the parable of the seeds. Most of the seeds fell on rocky, shallow, and thorny ground and did not grow. The other seed fell on good soul where it produced a crop up to one hundred times what was sown. When explaining the illustration, Jesus said, "But the seed falling on good soil refers to someone who hears the Word and understands it."[4] Understanding God's Word produces ownership as one learns how to live in Christ and make an impact for the Kingdom of God. I firmly believe that equipping a student with faith ownership before graduation is the only way to ensure that they make a healthy transition to life after high school. That process begins by helping students, not only hear the Word, but understand what it says, as they become a doer of God's Word.

---

[4] Matthew 13:23

## Chapter One Questions:

*Think about your transition after high school and determine why it was the way it was. Was your transition smooth and healthy, or was it difficult and challenging? Why?*

*How does a Christian teenager, with visible growth in his faith, struggle to the point of declining in maturity once he leaves home after graduation? In your experience, how would you answer that question?*

*What are some of the key factors you have observed for why you have observed students struggling during the transition after high school?*

*Why is it important to help a student make a healthy transition out of high school?*

*What are a few a take-away points from this chapter that you feel were most important to you and your ministry?*

## Chapter Two - The Gap Effects

The contrast in the life of a recent graduate the night before he/she moves away from home has always been an absurd phenomenon to me. I remember that transition in my own life very well. One day I was living under the roof of my parents. There was a delicious, balanced dinner on the table, my clothes were nicely washed and folded, and I had that comforting feeling of being at home. The next night, I was sitting in a small cinderblock dorm room, with half of my clothes still in a bag, and the question of where I might find food on a campus that I was still unfamiliar with. My network of friends had quickly gone from hundreds to a few new faces, and my freedoms went from a few to hundreds of opportunities. Within a span of hours, everything had changed.

Like all students in this situation, I was excited and feeling up for the challenge. More than turning a page and starting a new chapter of life, I felt more like I was deleting the previous chapter and re-writing a new one. No one really knew me on campus which was both a blessing and a curse. At the time I didn't know what I didn't know, and that was the core of my struggle. Later in this book, I will walk you through how to prepare students for this transition. A big part of that preparation involves helping them develop what I call their "transition plan'. I didn't have one of those at the time. Because of that, I fell victim to many bad decisions and wasted opportunities.

## Short Term Effects of this Transition

There are numerous effects that come with the struggles of faith during the transition after high school. Some of these effects are short term and others are longer lasting. In the next few pages, we will look at five common short term effects that produce negative results in the life of the student, often lasting for the next few years of that individual's life.

*1. They make new friends and join groups that don't support growth in their faith.*

This is often the first mistake that is made, especially in college. In college, everyone wants to make new friends and join the right groups. The pressure to do this is often so overwhelming for an incoming freshman that they make these critical decisions in the moment. The lasting result to this problem is that they fail to discover the importance for Christian accountability, fellowship, and community.

As I have already shared, this happened to me. When I started college, I joined a fraternity that was a large part of the reason I went to the university that I did. It was fun, and I enjoyed the process. However, it wasn't long before I realized that I was surrounded by a group of really great guys, but none of them expressed a desire to grow in Christ. That can be a real identity stealer, even for someone who once had a firm foundation of faith.

It is true that we become like the people we are around. Proverbs 13:20 confirms this truth with: "Walk with the wise and become wise, for a companion of fools suffers harm."

Years later I met Chris on his college campus. I recruited Chris to be a leader on my ministry team and eventually brought him on staff. Chris was loved by the high school students we served as he was beginning to feel a calling to full-time youth ministry after graduation. Chris' community became our college-aged leadership team and the college ministry at our church. The next year, Chris came to me and talked about joining the football team. As an outstanding athlete in high school, Chris had dreamed about playing college football. Those initial ambitions were squashed with a knee injury his senior year in high school, but as a college sophomore, Chris saw his opportunity reappear. I remember being apprehensive because I knew he could not serve in our ministry and play college football because of time constraints. Chris had spent a year developing in ministry and building relationships with high school boys, and I didn't want him to lose that opportunity. After he decided to play football, I encouraged him to stay connected to the college ministry so that he had a Christ-centered community to keep him grounded in his faith. In typical Chris-style, he dove deep into his new football career and was all-in. The team became his community, and I watched him drift further away from the Christian leader I loved. After one season of football, Chris had moved on again but unfortunately, was no longer living the life of someone that I could invite back onto the leadership of our ministry team. He had become like those in his football community, destroyed his witness, and became disqualified to serve in youth ministry.

## 2. *They compromise themselves morally and sexually without even knowing it.*

This is often a guaranteed result of living in a community that is not focused on growing together in Christ. Once the individual surrounds himself in the worldly culture, without staying grounded in a faith community, he will begin to do things that seem normal in that setting but are quite opposite from the lifestyle that he might have led in high school. Therefore, the young Christian becomes deceived and begins to forget who he is in Christ.

When you look at this for what it truly is, this is an identity issue. We know from verses like John 1:12 that when we receive Christ, we are a child of

God. As 2 Corinthians 5 puts it, in Christ we are new. Romans 6:6 reminds us that before we were a slave to sin, our body was ruled by sin, but in Christ that is not who we are anymore. Therefore, a believer who drifts back into that world of sin is not living in the identity of who they truly are. As John 15 informs us, if we abide with Christ and stay connected to the Vine, we will produce fruit, but apart from that connection we can do nothing. When a young Christian is no longer pursuing growth and maturity in her faith, she will begin to live apart from her Savior, and her lifestyle will seem synonymous with the world.

When we are not living the life we were created to live, we often begin to believe the new self is who we really are. My junior year in high school, I felt God was calling me to a life of full-time youth ministry. I had discussions about this with my parents and mentors and was on course to plug into ministry opportunities in college and prepare for this call. Before my freshman year of college was over, I had fully abandoned that calling and was interested in pursuing something less important. I remember being surprised at the reaction of my family and friends when I shared that revelation with them. The truth is, they knew who I really was, but I was believing the image that I saw of myself reflecting off of the life I was living.

### 3. *They allow peers and adults (friends, professors, etc.) to produce doubts in the faith they grew up with.*

When a teenager moves from an environment of faith to one of secular thinking, they begin to doubt the very truths that they once thought were firm. For most, this is usually the first time they have been challenged in this way, and they feel intimidated and unprepared for the conflict. The result is that they often begin to question themselves and the existence and truth of God.

In the 2014 movie God's Not Dead, Christian college freshman, Josh Wheaton, is challenged on the first day of his philosophy class. In the movie, his atheistic Professor Dr. Radisson informs the class that everyone will need to declare, in writing, the statement: "God is dead." When Wheaton refuses, the story takes the student and professor head to head to prove whether or not God exists. Even though this movie is fictionally based, the concept is very much alive in college classrooms all over the world. If doubt is not produced in the classroom, it most likely will be through conversations with peers or other influences.

While teaching this point to a group of youth ministry leaders a few years ago, I had a young leader comment about how healthy he believed doubts were in faith. My comment to him was that doubts are common and somewhat natural in our journey of faith, but according to Scripture, they are anything but healthy. In the Bible, we see that doubt is the opposite of faith and a partner with fear. Resolving doubts can make you stronger in your faith, but only when you have a solid foundation of faith to draw from. In James 1:6, faith that is filled with doubt can be washed away by a stormy sea. Instead, Romans 10:17 says that we have faith when we hear the Word of God. A student who is actively growing and maturing in God's Word will not be tossed around by challenges of faith. This is most often the case when the individual stays connected to Christian community and is living his identity in Christ for all to see.

4. *They are not involved in a local church.*
I am convinced that if I had found a church my freshman year in college that my story would have been considerably different. Christian community is important at any age, but during a life transition, it is critical. I have talked to many college students over the years who have been "church shopping" for four years. They periodically visit churches for years and never settle into one. The result of this is that they are not connected to the body of Christ and therefore, miss out on opportunities to worship, serve, and be discipled during some of the most formative years of their lives.

*Life is made up of a series of seasons with transitional periods in between. How one handles this first major life transition will effect the next one as well.*

I remember seeing one of my college-aged friends recently as he was home for the weekend. I asked him how school was going, and he said it was good. Then I asked him where he was going to church, and he said that he was coming home for church. Knowing that he was an hour from home and that he had not been home in months, I decided to ask again. He let me know that he started out the school year wanting to find a local church but then got busy. I have found that if someone is too busy for community, discipleship, and worship, then that individual has some major priorities out of order. Scripture is clear on the importance of being a part of the Body of Christ.

1 John 1:7 says that if we walk in the light that we will have fellowship with others walking in God's light. Galatians 6:2 urges believers to carry one another's burdens, and Proverbs 27:17 speaks to how community makes one another stronger. Your high school friends who are preparing for this transition must understand their need to be a part of a church. This is where they will find community, and as I have shown in this progressing list of short term effects, a lack of community opens the individual up to struggles and challenges he might not have had otherwise. As Hebrews 10:24-25 encourages us: "And let us consider how we may spur one another on toward love and good deeds, not giving up meeting together, as some are in the habit of doing, but encouraging one another."

### 5. They live a spiritually marginal life & focus their attention on insignificant, worldly issues.

This final short term effect is more of an end result to leaving the Christian influences of high school and not replacing them in the next chapter of life. In many cases, these teenagers stop pursuing growth in their relationship with Christ and fall further behind in the maturity needed to live out their call & purpose. Whereas they once were interested in missions and caring for others in the name of Jesus, they are now focused on cultural issues and political platforms that are widely popular among college-aged individuals. I could fill this book with examples of this from decades of watching it develop in students I have known.

One such example is John, a midwestern son of a pastor who grew up taking mission trips and teaching Bible studies. John then went to a large state university where he went down the traditional path of partying and casual sexual relationships. At one time, John was going to change the world for Christ. By the time he graduated from college his dream was to open a bar that had dog care facilities because, as he stated, one of the great needs in our society is for people to be able to come to a bar with their friends and know that their pets can have fun, too. If you ask me, it seems that John might have lost his kingdom-building perspective.

## Long Term Effects of this Transition

Those are just a few short term effects caused by a lack of spiritual growth and maturity during the transition after high school. Some of these situations affect the individual for a few years, and others might be affected for a much longer period of time.

A few years ago, a friend of mine asked a favor. He taught a Sunday School class at our church of young married couples, and because he had to be out of town one weekend, he asked me to fill in for him. I was excited because I rarely get to spend much time with that age group. The class was made up of about 20 couples, all ranging in age from about 23-29. All had only been married for approximately 1-5 years and only a few children. I shared with the class about my ministry to help high school students prepare their faith for the challenges and freedoms of college. I asked them to raise their hands if they felt that their faith struggled during that season of time. All hands went up. Curious about the lingering effects of this transition, I asked if anyone felt that they were still dealing with a faith maturity deficit that began when they transitioned out of high school. Most hands went back up. Knowing that these couples were a few years removed from this transitional stage, I asked if anyone wanted to share. One guy sitting with his wife on the back row shared that this was their second week back in church since high school. He said that they both grew up in the church but did not connect to a Christ-centered community in college. Once the couple began to date and later got married, they were no longer in the habit of going to church and therefore, did not. Four years removed from their college graduation, they decided that this was the missing link in their relationship. A young mother raised her hand to say that it wasn't until her daughter was born a few months ago that they realized the need to rededicate their lives to Christ and start growing in the faith that had lain dormant for so long. Another female raised her hand and tearfully shared that she had met a guy in college and married him the week after graduation. Within a year of getting married, the couple got divorced, and she admitted that if she had continued to focus on her relationship with Christ in college that she would have never dated and married that guy.

The long term effects of this transition can produce life long challenges. The reason for this is because of the stage of life in which they occur. Once an individual leaves home and begins life on his own, he begins to develop into the adult that he wants to be. He makes his own decisions as habits are formed out of the values and interests that he deems most important. This lifestyle builds upon itself as he gets older and usually is only tweaked as life changes settings. The long term effects of this transition include, but are certainly not limited to, years or even decades of spiritual dryness, broken relationships, sporadic church involvement, and a lack of purpose. These can in turn produce unfaithfulness in marriage and the workplace, a philosophy of worldly parenting, a lifestyle of sin management rather than total surrender, and a self-centered attitude of service and charity.

I believe that these effects are rarely traced back to this transition because they are camouflaged by how commonplace they are in the culture that we live in. We do not often hear of a couple's divorce, infidelity, or unethical act and connect the dots to their transition after high school, but if they grew up in a Christ-centered home and then strayed from that faith in the years after graduation, that connection may not be very far fetched.

I have talked with friends for many years that corroborate this claim. One such friend is Joseph who is married with three children. Joseph grew up in church and in a Christian family but, in his own words, spent decades going through the motions and playing a role of the happy Christian businessman and family man. After an affair, his world was rocked, and he finally saw the hypocrisy. When I asked him to think back on when things began to change and when his faith began to be less of a priority in his life, he quickly said that it began after he left home and went to college. He played college baseball and, again in his own words, did not have time for God. After graduation, Joseph made it his priority to climb the corporate ladder and make a name for himself. This went on for fifteen years until he was publicly fired for an office romance. Today, Joseph is a rock. The Lord gave him the strength (and his wife the grace) to save his marriage, and he is a mature follower of Christ. The wounds are still there, but Joseph is faithful to himself, his family, and most importantly, to his Savior.

I believe that the transition after high school is a pinnacle moment for individuals, where they will either continue to grow and mature, making an impact on the world, or struggle in their faith while becoming vulnerable to sin, unhealthy relationships, and rabbit-chasing detours in the pursuit of meaning and purpose. What your teenagers do not currently realize is that life is made up of a series of seasons with transitional periods in between. How one handles this first major life transition will affect the next one as well. When you address this transition with your high school seniors, they may only see it as your last ditch effort to help them follow Jesus in college, but it is so much more than that. We aren't just trying to help them find Christian friends in college and connect better as a freshman. We are trying to keep them from struggling with teenage sins as a thirty-year-old spouse and parent. We are teaching them how to develop a faith maturity that will help them keep a job, raise their kids in the church, and grow into a mature, Christ-centered man or woman of God, both as a college-age student and as a middle-age adult. That is what is at stake here.

# Chapter Two Questions:

What are some other short-term effects for a student struggling during this transition that were not mentioned in the chapter?

What are some other long-term effects for a student struggling during this transition that were not mentioned in the chapter?

Based on what you have always thought about common college transition struggles, how have your views strengthened or changed after reading this chapter?

What are a few take-away points from this chapter that you feel were most important to you and your ministry?

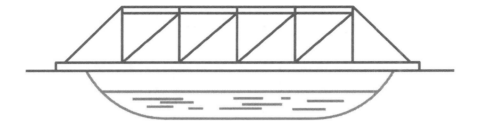

## Chapter Three - Adolescents in Transition

I have served in full-time student ministry since the mid-nineties. I have personally known hundreds of kids in a discipling capacity. I have sat down and opened up the Bible thousands of times with teenagers and discussed the Scriptures and how much God truly loves them. Throughout that process, I have seen some kids really get it. You can see the Spirit move and things begin to click. They discover who they are and begin to make sense of what it means to serve God and live in him. Likewise, I have seen others allow the truth of God to go in one ear and out the other. For those who get it, that's a huge first step; one of many on the road to spiritual maturity. But, for many kids that I have encountered over the past couple of decades, I have found that they are far from really getting it. They have been sprinkled with the Word but hardly got wet.

40

These teenagers regularly attend a worship event but have no conscious desire to worship. They show up to a Bible Study with little interest for studying the Bible. They come to camp for the games and go to the weekly events for the free pizza. They are products of an immature, generational mentality of "entertain me so I can have fun" rather than "challenge me so I can grow."

Ministry to adolescents is hard, as you already know. And I think that it might be even harder today than in generations past. Today, kids have far more distractions and influences than kids in my generation, or possibly yours, ever did. In my day, when I left the house, I walked away from media distractions; now those devices come with them in their pockets. When I was a teenager, my social life consisted of real conversations, face to face or at least voice to voice. Today that has all changed. Kids know more, and are expected to do more to be popular, relevant, and social. In this chapter, we are going to look deeper into the world of the kids that we are called to lead and disciple. Before we can bridge the gap in the transition after high school, we must first understand where adolescents are today and how we can attempt to lead them.

*Kids today are overly stressed, media saturated, relationally malnourished, over materialized, ADD defined, and often confused about who they are suppose to be.*

## The Evolution of the Adolescent

The evolution of the adolescent is an interesting one. When I say the word "adolescence," what age range do you think of? Some might say that it represents the teen years. Others might reduce that assumption or expand it a couple years on either side. The truth is, adolescence is less of an age range and more of a state of development. I described what I am about to tell you in my book to parents called *Ownership Road*, but I think it is important to recap this evolution of adolescence so that we can be reminded of the world current teenagers are living in.

The term adolescence is defined as the developmental period of time between childhood and adulthood, and prior to 1900, the word nor concept even existed. Before this time, there wasn't a period of development before becoming an adult. A person worked from a young age to help the family survive and then got married and started a family just after puberty. It wasn't until the turn of the 20th century that the term was first used, representing a very small window, ending at approximately 16 years old as public schools began to emerge and lengthened the stage of development. By the 1940's, and after the Great Depression and world wars, teenagers were no longer needed to work to help the family make a living and therefore had "free time" for the first time ever. It is also during this period that youth organizations, such as Young Life and Youth For Christ, began to provide age appropriate Christian activities for teenagers. By the 1960's, the stage of adolescence grew from a range of just a few years to represent all of the teenage years. It was during this time that more churches began hiring full-time staff to disciple and lead youth ministries. Today, and for the past couple of decades, the range of adolescence has widened as children are "growing up" much younger and yet also, "staying young" much longer. One could suggest that the current adolescent age range today could begin as early as 10 or 11, and continue through the mid twenties.

So, what does that really mean? Well, it can mean a lot when attempting to answer some of the questions in relation to teens and their environment. First, it means that many individuals are currently leaving home to live as adults while still respectively being adolescents, in the developmental sense of the word. They feel like adults, society is telling them that they are adults, yet they don't think or act like a mature adult. It also means that we must do a better job in the discipling process so that the students we are leading are developed enough to handle the challenges they will face on their own.

Kids today are overly stressed, media saturated, relationally malnourished, over materialized, ADD defined, and often confused about who they are suppose to be. It has become the norm to pile adult pressures on our kids. This is both a direct cultural influence as well as an indirect one from parents and other culturally consumed adults. According to one authority, approximately 60 percent of teenagers and 50 percent of "tweenagers" say that they are always on the edge of stress, citing reasons ranging from grades to weight and living in conflict with their parents; all on an average of five to six hours of sleep a night (2-4 hours below recommended).[5]

A few years ago I was speaking at a freshman orientation for a small Christian college with about 500 incoming freshmen in attendance. This orientation was held the week before classes started, so these students moved to campus and went straight to this "welcome week" before entering the classroom. During one session, I held a Q & A and I discovered that most of these new college students were already heavily stressed. They had moved away from home but had yet to take one day of a college class. They had not yet felt the demands of a college research paper or the social stress of roommates or rush. When I asked why they were stressed, many of them where concerned because they didn't know what they would major in, how they would make good enough grades to graduate, and how they would find a post-college job. They hadn't fully started college yet, and they were already scared to death about how they would finish. This is the mindset of a teenager today who has grown up in a post-9/11 world with a struggling economy, failing marriages all around, and high social demands to stay in school so the world of Facebook doesn't find out that you failed out and work at Burger King. The teenagers you lead are 75% adult and 25% kid by the age of 16 in what they know, what is expected, and the huge mountain that they feel required to climb. Kids today are often forced to practice hours a day for youth sports and study as long as it takes to get an A. They are pressured much more than they can handle, leaving them to live an

[5] *When Kids Hurt: Help for Adults Navigating the Adolescent Maze*, Chap Clark, Baker Books, 2009, page 131-132

overly stressed pre-adult life. Then, they crash on the couch and consume TV and video games for the rest of the day. According to the Kaiser Family Foundation, kids spend an average of 8 hours on media a day, with over half of that time watching television. It is no wonder kids are starving from a lack of personal interaction and dealing with identity issues.

## Three Categories of Students in Transition

In my years of working with teenagers, I have seen many examples of how recent high school graduates struggle in the months and years to follow. I have watched as some make choices that they never would have made in high school. For others, the warning signs began to come to light in high school and yet were not fully exposed until the individual was out of the house and able to flex those freedom muscles. Without trying to put teenagers into labeled boxes, I would like to suggest three general categories that I have observed among professing Christian teenagers who struggle in life and faith after high school. I think it might be helpful to begin thinking of which of your students fit into these categories as you read through the descriptions.

First, we have what I call **The Bubble Popper**. This is an individual who has grown up in somewhat of a strict household. This is often someone who was forced to go to church at every opportunity yet never truly connected relationally with that community. Church became something that the Bubble

Popper dreaded by the time he or she was in the last few years of high school. This might not be apparent by the time the student got to church on Sunday mornings, but the sentiment was there both before and after in his mind and heart. The Bubble Popper often found himself socially torn by the friends who were considered the popular "party crowd" and the faith that he was expected to live. This faith is most likely immature, or possibly even non-existent, yet the majority of people would not know that because of the Popper's family, his activities, and a proper outward behavior. Secretly, the Bubble Popper is looking forward to the next chapter of life after graduation being everything that high school wasn't. He declares that he is tired of being the "good guy," and therefore graduates from high school, moves away from home, and pops the bubble that he had made his home for far too long.

I have known so many Bubble Poppers over the years. Some popped the bubble before graduation, but whenever it happened, their new behavior was almost always a huge surprise to the parents, teachers, and mentors who never saw it coming. Do you have any Bubble Poppers in your ministry right now? Chances are you can think of some that are both in your ministry now as well as those who have moved on. I want to encourage you to write their name or initials on this page so that you can begin to determine how to best lead them.

So, how do we help Bubble Poppers transition well? First, I think we help them to open up as we define for them some of the misconceptions of a lukewarm faith. I think we also help them to feel valued, nurtured, and appreciated in your ministry group. A Bubble Popper may only be there out of obligation or requirement, so surprise him or her with a responsibility that gives them meaning and purpose in the group. The Bubble Popper often will respond well to a solid senior transition initiative, especially if the student is planning to go to college. The key for them will be to begin seeing the importance of faith in that transition. This type of student needs to be given one on one time to sit across the table over coffee or milkshakes as a friendship develops between student and mentor. First, this student needs some time to open up and identify the barriers he has put up in his faith. He needs to understand the value of community and his need for the church now and in the future. If church is just an obligation after high school, the need for Christian community will become obsolete in college. Therefore, to fully prepare the Bubble Popper for this transition, he needs to go back to the basics of faith first, reconnect to an active and growing relationship with Jesus, and begin to understand how to transition that faith to the next stage of life.

The second category of transitional struggles comes from **The Fence Rider**. The Fence Rider, unlike the Bubble Popper, is someone who grew up in a laid-back home environment. Sometimes a chip off of the old block, the Fence Rider rides the fence of moral and social behavior. This is the teen who came to church for the social opportunities and was not ashamed of the fading scent of alcohol still lingering from the night before. The Rider's parents are often more concerned with their child's success than her faith, as religion is a piece of the family puzzle, but not the center. To be fair, I have found the Fence Rider to be very genuine and honest. This is not an individual who is hiding behind a bubbled wall and is often someone that would be an incredibly bright light in the world if she truly understood what it meant to follow Jesus in high school.

But for now, The Fence Rider is expecting the next stage of life to be as socially and spiritually lackadaisical as high school was as she rides the fence of faith, enjoying both sides of an opportunity.

I have also known many Fence Riders in my years of ministry. Often, if the parent is aware of this position, they usually are either okay with it or unsure how to change it. I have even known parents of Fence Riders to think of their child as more of a Bubble Popper. It is a fair assessment that the faith of a Fence Rider is not of importance to the individual at the time of their transition out of high school, but many of my friends over the years who went on to be amazing Christian leaders and mentors to teenagers were at one time Fence Riders in high school.

So, how do we reach a Fence Rider? First, we lay out a lot of grace. A pointing finger will send the student to go ride someone else's fence. We don't want that. Again, we must find the time to share a table at the coffee house or taco bar, and we talk. As they lay out how they see the world, often open-minded Fence Riders will listen honestly to your point of view. These students are only living this lifestyle because they haven't fully experienced a true encounter with Jesus. I have found that one of the best ways to counter this is to expose the Rider to the world outside of himself as you serve together and even do ministry together. I have even invited a musical Fence Rider to play guitar and lead worship, along side of me. This always brings a rise out of the Pharisee teens in the room, but is a total Jesus-move and gives purpose to the Rider that they are a part of the body. A Fence Rider can make a healthy transition to college if he sees the importance of faith, community, and service in that new setting.

I think overall there are three things we can do for both of these types of students. First, we love them. When I say that, I know you already love them, so what I mean is you make your love known to them. In a culture where there is a string attached to everything, be that unconditional friend. Call them up, not to ask them to do something or to come to something, but just to see how their day was. Take a genuine interest in them, in a way that no one else is probably doing. This will go a long way with your Poppers and Riders. I learned years ago that a key step in relational ministry is to first earn the right to be heard. This means we must first build the trust of a friendship before that relationship can have a discipleship component to it.

Secondly, keep it relevant while keeping it simple. This is the art of ministry. Few things in the world of a teenager are truly meaningful. The games they play never end, the shows they watch leave them hanging, and the expectations to perform leave them empty. So make everything count in your ministry efforts, but keep it simple.

So, love them, keep it relevant and simple, and then make a difference together. So many youth ministries talk about serving and yet never serve. Or, the only time they serve is on a big far away mission trip with only those who have the time and money to go (an adventure that you might not even have any Fence Riders go on, by the way). When given the chance to grow by serving and giving their life away, your students will feel a weight lifted as the attention is taken off of them and put on someone else. This will give them the perspective that Jesus wants us to have in order to love our neighbor. It is the essence of following Jesus, and those experiences can help mold them into the compassionate, selfless servant of Christ that they were created to be.

Finally, we have **The Current Coaster.** This is the teenager whose faith struggle is the most surprising to all who know her. This is the one of the three that my transition story best fits in. Unlike the Bubble Popper and Fence Rider, the Current Coaster is raised in a spiritually nurturing environment. She is not only active in her church but recognized as a leader in her faith both at church and school. The Current Coaster often takes advantage of mission and ministry opportunities and has solid positive influences in her life from peers to mentors. Because of her faith maturity, the Current Coaster's life resembles an afternoon of floating down a river on an inner tube where she only has to hang on and enjoy the ride. She knows where to go for community, accountability, discipleship, and mentoring. All of those relationships are firmly set by the Coaster's senior year in high school; and therefore, she can just easily coast through her years of high school without having to paddle.

What no one has realized is that the Coaster has never learned how to grow in her faith without those guiding influences in her life. Therefore, this spiritual drift produces a false sense of maturity for the Current Coaster. Believing that she has mastered the art of avoiding peer pressure, she expects to continue to coast through college on the same waves as high school, only to find herself up a creek when she realizes that the currents flow differently after high school. Current Coasters seem to be doing so well in high school and then appear to "lose themselves" after they are on their own, due to the contrast.

So, how do you help the Current Coaster prepare for the transition to life after high school? First, you help them understand the difference in being a Christian (in society) and following Jesus. Depending on the individual, the Coaster might be living the moral life of a Christian without living for Jesus. If this is the case, the fall after leaving home is understandable. Therefore, like the other two, you must assess the student's level of maturity and disciple accordingly so that the teen understands what it means to follow Jesus and live for Him. Secondly, you continue to give your Coasters leadership roles in your ministry which, by their senior year, you would do naturally. Helping these students lead will give them a greater purpose in ministry. Then, you help the Current Coaster create a plan for transitioning that purpose of ministry into the next stage of life.

The truth is, all three of these types of struggling teenagers have one thing in common: a failure to prepare well. Granted, by their senior year in high school, the Bubble Popper and Fence Rider may not want to prepare, but, never the less, preparation for transitioning one's faith from the nurturing environment of home to a life away is critical.

So, now that we have established that most Christian teenagers struggle because they are not prepared for the challenges of life on their own, that brings up a very important question: How do we prepare these students? That is the direction we are headed in the remaining chapters of this book. Next, we will look at the role of the ministry leader, and then we can begin to focus on the plan for preparing them for life after high school, first looking through a wide lens and then narrowing that focus with a senior initiative and freshman follow-up plan.

## Chapter Three Questions:

What are some ways in which you have changed your approach to ministry over the year/years to adjust to the changing world of adolescents?

Who do you know in your current ministry who could be identified as each of the categories presented, and how can you specifically reach out to those individuals to help them grow, mature, and eventually transition?

Bubble Popper:

Fence Rider:




Current Coaster:




What are few a take-away points from this chapter that you feel were most important to you and your ministry?

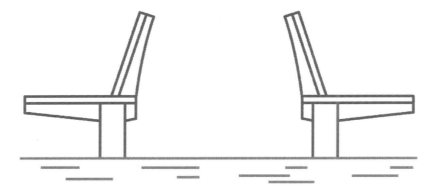

## Chapter Four - Transitional Discipleship

In Luke 15, Jesus tells the parable of the lost son. This story, possibly better named the parable of the two lost sons, is very appropriate for this transitional issue. The younger son has enough of house and home , so he packs up the Mustang (maybe literally) and he leaves. Ready or not, distant country, here he comes. Assured of himself, he sets off with half of his father's wealth to support himself. His plan? Jesus doesn't say, but I can only guess that he packed the Playstation, some Gatorade, and plenty of Ramen Noodles for the journey ahead. Not long after he gets to his destination, he spends all that he has on "wild living." Now, armed with nothing but his pride, he searches for a job, but because of a famine, all he can find is work in the pig fields. He is even reduced to eating the pig's food, apparently because he ran out of both pride and noodles. Then, in verse 17, we see something beautiful. It says that the son, who has hit rock bottom, finally "comes to his senses". He gets to a point in his life where he begins to notice that the life he once had is more fulfilling than his current situation. He understands that he has made a mistake and, as we learn in the following verses, is now willing to do whatever it takes to go back to his father. To the younger son, the father says, "For this son of mine was dead and is alive again; he was lost and is found" (verse 32).

The truth is, your students are going to graduate from high school, go to college or to a job, and exercise some level of freedom. In so many ways, they need to do that. We hope they don't find themselves eating with the pigs. Rather, we hope that once they get there and see how hard it's going to be, they come to their senses about who they are and what they have been created for. But, you can't come to your senses unless you have a sense to come back to, and that is our job as leaders, mentors, and those called to guide students by helping them strengthen their foundation that they can rely on during a season of life when everything else is shifting.

## Your Ultimate Goal in Ministry

Let me ask you a question that I think may be the most important point of this conversation: *What is your ultimate goal for the students in your ministry?* What is it that you wake up every morning hoping to achieve through your ministry? I know you hope all of your students will follow Jesus. I know that you also want them to understand the command to love God with their all, and to love their neighbors as they love themselves. You hope to teach them God's Word and how to apply it to the world around them. You want them to enjoy community and fellowship and make right decisions by using wisdom. Your heart would no doubt burst at the idea of your students hearing a call to ministry and developing a Christ-centered purpose for their life. I know that these are all goals you have, but the bigger question is: What is your *ultimate* goal for the students in your ministry?

I would like to propose an answer for you to that question. I believe that your ultimate goal for your students in your ministry is to equip them with enough faith ownership before they graduate from high school so that they can stand on their own two feet in their faith and handle the challenges that the next stage of life offers. I say this because you are a stage ministry. You have these young people for most of their teen years, but then they are gone. You have them in middle and high school, but you will not have them forever. Therefore, just as a children's ministry should prepare the faith of kids for the teen years, you should set a goal to prepare the faith of your students for the college-aged years. It is not your role, per se, to equip them for marriage, parenthood, middle age, etc, but rather to prepare them in such a way that they can handle the pressures of life after graduation with wisdom, love, and faithfulness.

Now, as a follow-up question: how does that change the way you do ministry? What would you do differently if you thought about your goal of preparing them in their faith for the next stage of life? I would think that this would change everything. If this was your goal, then everything you do with your students should point back to that goal. Every trip, every study, every service opportunity, everything should be a lesson in how to live in maturity with Christ once they are on their own.

As someone who focuses on this transition full-time, I spend much of my weekly conversations with youth ministry leaders. I love to hear how a leader is approaching their calling of leading kids closer to Jesus. At some point in the conversation, I always ask one particular question: *"What have you done well, or seen done well, to prepare a student for the challenges of life after high school?"* This isn't intended to stump the youth pastor or shine a light on a weak link, but rather to provide me with a point of reference to know how to help. Usually I get a lot of "Um...well... Ah... Yeah... Well... We...uh...we tried something, can't remember now, um, not much." Every once in a while I get an answer that is well communicated and thorough, but not often.

In my experience, I typically get one of three general responses to my question. The first is when the youth worker says that they spend a few weeks in the spring addressing the issues of the transition and covering the key topics during that study. Ironically, these are the same leaders that "um, uh" their way through answering my question. To me, I hear that this leader's plan is to approach, arguably, the most critical and life-altering transition in the teen's life by spending a collective four to five hours preparing for it. This is very common and often yields mixed results.

Once, a student pastor responded by saying, "We use your book," meaning my book for seniors, *Lost in Transition*. I asked, "Great! How did it go?" He admitted that they intended to teach the book but never got around to it. Incidentally, they simply passed out the books and never even followed up to see if the students had read it on their own (which usually doesn't happen).

*What have you done well, or seen done well, to prepare a student for the challenges of life after high school?*

The second most popular answer that I get is that the church plans an end-of-the-year senior recognition event where the parents and students eat a meal, receive a gift, and hear a lasting send-off speech. I have spoken at many of these type of events, and they usually always include smiles, tears, cheesecake, and a slideshow of embarrassing baby pictures. These events are great to reflect on the memories and celebrate the student, but the problem comes when this is your answer to my question of how you are preparing students for this transition. I hope that every church is hosting some kind of senior celebration for graduates, while also understanding that those events do very little to prepare students for the challenges ahead.

The third, and most troubling answer I get is: "We don't do anything because we don't have any seniors." Now, if one comes from a young church that started with a few young families and the oldest teenagers are in the 7th grade, I understand not having seniors. But, if a church doesn't have seniors because they have all left, something is seriously wrong with the vision of the student ministry and of the larger church as a whole.

So, let's look at these three responses. First, let's take Mark, for example. Mark is a youth pastor that I've worked with who started taking his seniors through a month long study in April each year with little participation or impact. When he and I first spoke, he was worn down and frustrated. I could tell that Mark was trying and honestly doing the best he knew how to do, but when he began the study each year, the seniors had already begun to check out and were no longer tracking with what he was teaching. This would become evident each fall of the next year as he followed up with some of those students and determined that they did not retain much of what was discussed in April. As I told Mark, seniors already float through that last year barely conscious in the first place, therefore, waiting until late spring to summarize a faith-filled life in college in four, one-hour sessions, is not going to yield a strong return.

Jim is also a youth pastor and plans a huge Senior Sunday event every spring at his church where the whole day is dedicated to celebrating seniors. Like many churches, students get invited back on this day that haven't been seen in a while, so that they can be sent off. For those students, they didn't even get the four-weeks-in-April study. They have been in and out of church throughout high school and now get to be congratulated and well-wished. The truth is a Senior Sunday is not a post-high school transition plan, which needs to include training and discipleship, not just recognizing. I meet a lot of ministry leaders like Mark and Jim.

Then there is Sam. Sam is the one who looks across the table at me and says that he doesn't have any seniors by the time the school year gets underway. He admits that they begin to fade away during their junior year, while leaving the remaining few to check out after the summer activities. He wrote this off on busy schedules and the demands of trying to get into college, but usually the reasons are much deeper and harder to identify. As I shared with Sam, here are three main reasons that I have found why kids drift away from church by their senior year.

First, sometimes the apparent drop-out rate for older students in church has little to do with the teenager, but rather concerns the family. If the family is not active in church, the kids are often going to follow suit. If the family moves, changes churches, or buys a weekend house at the beach, attendance and involvement is going to be affected. Once a youth pastor told me that his senior pastor questioned him about the declining numbers in the youth group. The truth was that the once thriving ministry that took a hundred to retreats was now looking into a few dozen faces instead. Wisely, and boldly, the student pastor noted to his boss that the rate of decline of the student ministry was actually slightly less than that of the overall church decline. If there are fewer students in your youth ministry than a year or two ago, the first place you might want to look is the church-wide attendance roll.

A second reason is that the student has begun to let go of everything connected to high school life and is mentally and emotionally focused on what comes after graduation. We call this Senioritis, where a senior has given up on high school life and refuses to function in life until he can do so in the setting of college. This is an immature, undisciplined approach to life, but it is real and we see it every year. I have looked in the eyes of many high school seniors and seen the desperation of just wanting to be gone from the high school life they have grown tired of. I've had Christian, church kids tell me that they are tired of being good, of playing the role of the Christian of *that* family, in *that* church, from *that* school. They want nothing more than to go to college and live life the way they want to live it. Sometimes in response to this, parents let go of the rope and let their student begin to make more of his own decisions. The parents recognize that their child will have total freedom next year anyway, and thinks: why not start now? This is not a reflection on you or your ministry personally, but there are ways that you can help the student. This reaction is a symptom of a great void of maturity in the life of the teenager, and any influence that you can have in his or her life at that moment may produce fruit.

The third reason why kids drift away from the church by the senior year is because they are tired of the same old youth group experience that they have been involved in for the past four to six years. Often times the youth group schedule can become routine and predictable after a student gets to his junior or senior year. He has gone to one too many lock-ins, progressive dinners, and nursing home service projects. He wants to be away at college, and the church youth experience is "so high school". This *is* a reflection of your ministry, and later in this book we will look at ways to make the senior year unique and different enough that students will look forward to becoming a senior in your ministry.

My advice to Sam, Jim, Mark, and yourself is to think differently when it comes to leading seniors. Why? ...because they are different. They are the oldest students that you have in your middle and high school ministry; they are beginning to deal with more adult world scenarios than any of your other students; and they are preparing to be on their own within 12 months from now. They are different, and they need to be led differently.

The students in your ministry are most likely not going to be naturally prepared to automatically leave all the influences of their faith and step into a path of maturity on their own, away from home. I believe that your job is to partner with the parents to strengthen the foundation of your students so that they can leave home fully equipped to live and lead as the light of the world. Just like any ministry effort, this mission focus takes intention, wisdom, authentic communication, and dedicated discipling. If you have worked in youth ministry for more than a day, you probably already knew that. Chances are, when it comes to this transition, you do not struggle with the question of "why", instead your problem is "how", "when", and "what." The purpose of this book, and my ministry in general, is to help you develop those answers in such a way that fits into the ministry that you have already developed.

# Transitional Discipleship

Think about the top two or three most important faith components that you think your students need to have grasped before they move away from your ministry and write them in the margin of this page. I will mention the first couple that come to my mind: community and church involvement. Your list might be different from mine, and that's okay. Now, how are they going to develop these faith principles and components? Are you being intentional about teaching these things, or do you hope they grab hold of them as they pass by? I think you have to be intentional, or they won't get the point. For example, they know that you hope they continue to be involved in a church in college, but do they know how that process works? Do they know the value of the church in their lives and what Scripture says about the purpose of the church? It is not enough that they are present every weekend at church in high school; that could be because there is an expectation of them coming from their parents. That is not a guarantee that they will be active in church after they leave home, far from it.  Are your students going to connect the dots from having community in high school (the youth group) to finding new community after graduation (college-aged ministry)? They probably will not because they did very little to form that high school community as it developed around them automatically. Many college students go to a new campus and subconsciously think that will happen again in the same way, but it rarely does. This is why you must have this goal in your mind and seek out opportunities to teach them these principles. They must learn that one day soon they will have to find a new church that will serve as their church home and provide community while they are away from home.

This perspective of student ministry is what I call **Transitional Discipleship**. This is the approach of discipling your middle and high school students with this transition in mind. If you have a traditional ministry structure at your church, your students will leave your ministry after they graduate. This means you can look at every one of your students and basically predict how much longer you have with each of them. Then, you have to determine what you will teach them to prepare them for this transition and how you will incorporate that into the day-to-day of your ministry.

## Student Exit Strategy

The first step of Transitional Discipleship is to develop your student exit strategy. If I asked you what your student exit strategy is, what would you say? I once asked a youth pastor that question, knowing that this was a new concept that he would not understand immediately, and he looked at me and then said, "I'll probably do this for a little while longer and then move on." I laughed and said, "Not your 'personal exit from the church' plan, but your strategy for how you will best prepare your students to leave your ministry equipped for the next stage of life." A student exit strategy is an end goal expectation for each teenager for what they will take with them when they graduate from high school and leave your student ministry. This question challenges the very core of your ministry mission purpose and serves as a reminder of the opportunity we have been given to develop the young faith of teenagers during this very formative season of life.

When you think in terms of a youth ministry's student exit strategy, you must first look at the end and determine the most important thing that a student needs in order to continue growing and maturing in the next season of life. To determine this, you must ask yourself a few questions. First, what kind of challenges will students face after they leave high school? Secondly, what faith principles will they need to overcome those challenges and thrive at the next level? What will it take to help them grow and mature to the point that they can handle those challenges and continue on a trajectory of faith in life? As I have already mentioned, for me that one thing they need to develop can be summed up in the word: ownership. Again, ownership is the process of caring for and protecting something because it is very dear to you. When you have ownership over your faith, you pursue community, accountability, and discipleship opportunities to grow, develop, and mature. There is no possible way to continue maturing in faith after moving away from all the spiritual influences of high school if a teenager does not develop faith ownership, which is not going to happen automatically. So, for me, that is the end goal for a senior as he or she graduates from high school, to have visible signs of ownership in life and faith.

# Chapter Four Questions:

Do a self-evaluation for your past senior transition plan:

What was the end goal of the plan?

What were the strengths & weaknesses of the plan?

What was the fruit of the plan (how well did your students transition out of high school)?

What has been your experience in why seniors have drifted away from church involvement or dropped out all together by their senior year?

Why do you think that it is important to develop a detailed student exit strategy?

What are a few take-away points from this chapter that you feel were most important to you and your ministry?

## Chapter Five - The Ownership Wheel

My friend Carter grew up in a Christian home, but when he and I met his freshman year in high school, he was most interested in being liked and popular. Carter spent two years trying to be something he was not and finally found himself on a summer camp trip, with me, before his junior year. His life changed. He began to follow Jesus and live his life as the light of the world. For the next two years of high school, I discipled Carter weekly and prepared him for college. I knew that he had the pure gifts of ministry, with the compassion and humor to go along with it, but I had also seen him try to be the party kid and knew that he could easily fall back into that role in college. My goal, as he started his senior year in high school, was to help him see that he had a calling on his life. I knew that if Carter could see a glimpse of what I saw in him, he would go to college and be the light of the world. So, throughout his senior year, we studied Scripture, talked about calling, and I gave him opportunities to serve. Once he graduated and went on to college, he joined a fraternity so that he could make a difference there and also started training to be a Young Life leader. Over the years we met and shared a few meals together and talked about his ministry. He began his freshman year meeting with a few ninth grade boys in a small group Bible study. By the time Carter got to his senior year, those boys were seniors also. He texted me that summer and said he was on the bus heading to summer camp with those boys. A week later he texted me again to say that they were on the ride home and that two of his five guys decided to follow Jesus that week. It was like a lightning bolt of blessing straight to my heart. God will use your teenage friends in college for great things, and he is calling you to play a role in equipping them.

In the last chapter, I challenged you to adopt the perspective of Transitional Discipleship and to begin developing an exit strategy for your students. You may cover all of your students with one general strategy of equipping them with faith ownership before graduation. Or, you might be in a position to give them each a specific strategy like I was able to do with my friend Carter. Regardless of how specific you can get with each teenager, you need to take that exit strategy and begin to put arms and legs on it. This can happen as you fill in the Ownership Wheel.

The Ownership Wheel is a twelve progressional step process to help you organize the content you will teach as you lead your students to a place of

ownership. If you are familiar with some of my content for parents, this is similar to my "5 steps down the path from followship to ownership" in the book *Ownership Road.*

The twelve parts of The Ownership Wheel represent a progression of content you can teach to help kids reach a level of ownership before they leave your ministry. There are twelve parts to the wheel so that this can easily fit into an annual calendar for discipleship. I will give you the twelve discipleship topics that I have put on my wheel and give you the option to add/subtract or move them around as you finalize your wheel. Feel free to write them in on the wheel at the top of this page, beginning with the space that is on top, right of center (1:00), moving clockwise.

First, on The Ownership Wheel, I suggest that you start with *Jesus*. If you never teach your students anything else, teach them about Jesus. He is the author and perfecter of our faith (Hebrews 12:2). He is the centerpiece of our salvation story and the reason we have any hope of purpose or a future. You are going to want your students to know the stories of Jesus, to understand the parables of Jesus, and to feed on his Word, instruction, and grace. Your teenagers need to know Jesus and know what it truly means to follow him.

So many people have received the Jesus inoculation. They raised their hand, walked an isle, prayed a prayer, and got the Jesus salvation shot in the arm. Done! Now back to life. But, Jesus desires a relationship. Jesus wants us to follow him through life. He never says it will be easy. He never promises that he will lead to the prosperous life or even the safe life. He just says follow him, and he will give us life to the full (John 10:10b). Your kids need to know that, first and foremost. Anything less than that, and they will leave home thinking that Jesus is a religion rather than a relationship.

From there we move to the second step which represents *Identity in Christ*. Once a believer knows what it means to follow Jesus, he needs to begin seeing himself through that identity. We develop perspective in life from our identity and, as we know, perspective is very important when forming new friends, establishing a new direction in life and making important decisions on one's own. Scripture tells us who we are in Christ. Looking at 2 Corinthians 5 alone, we see that in Christ we are a new creation, called to be His Ambassador,

71

and because of Christ's death we have been made the righteousness of God. Understanding this is paramount in helping your students develop faith ownership. Our world is very identity-confused, and teenagers hear many voices trying to tell them who they want them to be. I have known so many teenagers who have grown up in the church but then graduate, leave that influence, and wander around life, questioning who they are and what they are suppose to be. According to the book of James, Scripture is our mirror where we see who we are in the reflection of God's Word (James 1:23-24).

Once identity is determined, we can begin to see the importance of a *Christ-focused Community*. For a teenager, community develops gradually over the years and might seem to just come together and fall into place for many high school students. But, for a high school graduate who leaves those friends and must seek new ones, that task can seem daunting and create a lot of questions about the need for a Christian community and for accountability. Depending on the individual's maturity, they may or may not know how to find a Christ-focused community, because they possibly never had to be intentional about it before. We must not only teach them the value and importance of community and accountability, but also the process for how to find a new community during a transition of life.

If anyone, teenager or adult, surrounds herself in the right community, she will automatically develop a genuine love for the church. The church is the body of Christ, and we are made to be in community with one another in fellowship, accountability, and love. Developing a love for the church is the next part of this Ownership Wheel. This is the essence of being one with Christ, and your students will need to grasp the purpose and value of a church community before leaving home, so that they feel the void and are compelled to replace that guiding influence.

So, we have come from loving Jesus to finding our identity in Christ, to connecting to a Christ-centered community and developing a *Love for the Church*. Once someone truly loves the church, he or she will truly learn to love worship. That is step five on my Wheel. Worship is our response to God for the goodness and graciousness that he gives. It is often not until we live in community and share each other's burdens that we understand what worship looks like. For most teenagers, "worship" is a 15 minute sing-a-long before someone gets up to preach. That is not worship, and the deeper we get into community, the more they will understand that.

Next is to become *Biblically Sound*. This is foundational for any believer and just as easily could have been placed second or third on the list before or after identity. We learn who we are through the Word, but so often it is not until people dive deep into community and the church, and discover true worship in their lives that they develop a longing to know and be in God's Word. David writes that the Word is a light to our feet, and Paul reminds us that the Word is used for "teaching, rebuking, correcting and training in righteousness." The author of Hebrews says that the Word is "living and active and sharper than any two-edged sword." Teenagers need to know Scripture. Imagine a star athlete attempting to play his position without first reading the playbook. The Bible is a playbook for how to live life fully. We have too many kids and adults in our churches who are trying to run the routes without knowing the plays.

Sometimes, just for fun, I like to ask a group of life-long church attending Christian teenagers what their favorite Bible verse is. Usually, and I mean almost always, someone says Jeremiah 29:11. Many times they don't even know the reference, instead they just say, "That verse about God knowing my plans to prosper me and not harm me." They are always shocked when I inform them that this verse says that God indicates the plan for His people would be fulfilled after they live in exile for 70 years. The students are usually dumbfounded. "No, not that verse, the one about God having a plan of hope for my life," they might say. Then I read the passage: "This is what the Lord says: 'When seventy years are completed for Babylon, I will come to you and fulfill my good promise to bring you back to this place. For I know the plans I have for you,' declares the Lord, 'plans to prosper you and not to harm you, plans to give you hope and a future. Then you will call on me and come and pray to me, and I will listen to you. You will seek me and find me when you seek me with all your heart. I will be found by you,' declares the Lord, 'and will bring you back from captivity. I will gather you from all the nations and places where I have banished you,' declares the Lord, 'and will bring you back to the place from which I carried you into exile.'" This little exercise is not to belittle students but to say that knowing Scripture is different from knowing about Scripture. Everyone wants the verse 11 hope and prosperity without the 70 year exile in Babylon. The truth is, sometimes God allows us to

*If you never teach your students anything else, teach them about Jesus. He is the author and perfecter of our faith.*

74

go to Babylon with a promise to protect us, and the better we know Scripture, the better we understand God's Will. Knowing Scripture helps us know God and our place in God's mighty plan. We can understand our circumstances, struggles, and even our successes fully when we know the Word of God. I am convinced that the deeper an individual's knowledge of Scripture is, the more joyful his life will be. This needs to be a priority to students preparing for this important transition.

After becoming Biblically sound, it is a natural next step to want to serve others in *Christ-like Service*. The Bible instructs us to love God with all our heart, soul, mind, and strength and love our neighbor as our self. That represents our defining pursuit as a follower of Jesus. The way to flesh that out into life is to serve others by loving them, giving to them, and putting them first. All of these ideas come from God's Word and flow against the current of our very nature as a human being living in the world. This isn't natural for our culture to put others first; and therefore, it has to be taught and caught. We need to give teenagers the opportunity to serve, but also to teach them why we serve and let them see that service as a command and a calling.

The summer before my senior year in college, I spent part of the summer in Russia on a mission trip. It was so life changing that I could spend hours telling you how God moved. But, that was not my first mission trip. I went on a few in high school and one other after my freshman year in college. The more someone is exposed to missions, the more committed they will become to the calling of God to serve others.

Once teenagers begin to see their lives as one that gives to others, it will open their eyes to a world in need. This represents the next step on the wheel: a *Christ-centered Worldview*. How we see the world is an extension of our identity and perspective in life, and worldview is a critical point on the Ownership Wheel. It represents an accumulation of a love for Jesus, an identity founded in Christ, being surrounded in community, understanding the purpose of the church and placing worship to God as a primary need in life. It's understanding Scripture and learning to serve others that helps us see the world as Jesus sees it. A Christ-centered worldview is the result of having the loving eyes of Christ for the broken world that we live in. It is being able to see things as they are and not as culture defines them, and knowing the difference between a wise decision and a foolish one. Everyone will develop a worldview. We want the students we lead to see the world in such a way that they want to serve it rather be served by it.

After a Christ-centered worldview is in place, a Christian can begin to learn how to defend what they believe through *Apologetics*. They know what the Word says and can therefore answer against challenges to the Truth. Then, they will be equipped to stand up for social and cultural issues. This means that your teenagers will need to learn about controversial issues and understand what Scripture says about them. For this, you might pick a few hot topics in the news or the most prominent on a college campus. You might consider a mock debate or an assignment where students have to research the argument and be prepared to offer a defense. This is so important in college because of the academic breeding ground for doubt that exists on a college campus.

The next step on the Ownership Wheel is developing a *Christ-like*

*Character*. Just like learning to be Biblically sound, this topic could go in a number of different places on the wheel. I like it in this spot because of all that goes into character development. The more one knows about walking with Jesus, an identity in Christ, community, Scripture, worship, serving, and apologetics, the more committed that individual will be to pursuing the character of Christ. These character traits can best be taught by looking into the Fruit of the Spirit in Galatians 5. Many of these qualities may already be present in a believer that has taken this process seriously, which will be an advantage at this stage of the Ownership Wheel.

Once a teenager learns about developing the character of Christ, he/she will naturally learn what it means to be a leader. I hope all Christian teenagers would develop into leaders because our world needs more Christ-centered leaders.  Culture, and sometimes even the church, has lost its focus on *leadership* development. We have become so individualized that the norm is to lead yourself rather than band together and lead and be led by others. As I have this goal for my own children, a strong leader will stand out, like a city on a hill. We just need to make sure that our leaders are leading in the right direction. Once a teenager gets to this place in the Ownership Wheel, he or she will be in a position to lead well, directly toward Jesus.

This brings us to the last space on the wheel which is *Ownership* in life and in faith. A teenager that grasps ownership in his or her life will have the confidence, wisdom, courage, grace, power, and authority to stand up and be an ambassador for Jesus Christ in a world that needs Him desperately. That is our end goal. We are in the business of making disciples and training ambassadors.

This is our mission, and this wheel illustration represents an exit strategy for our teenage friends that prepares them to thrive in life after they leave home and begin life on their own.

So now, you may be asking, "This sounds great but what do I do with it?" As I alluded to before, the Ownership Wheel has twelve parts so that it can easily fit into a calendar year of discipleship. I am not suggesting that you spend a year taking your seniors through the Ownership Wheel. By the time your students reach the twelfth grade, you will not have the time you need to adequately teach these principles and have them stick. Rather, I am suggesting that you start with your youngest group, possibly your sixth or seventh graders, and you begin to structure your discipleship efforts with them, using the wheel as your guide. This long-term approach came to me after I met a mother named Rose.

I got a call one Monday morning from Rose. I had never met Rose, but she was a friend of a friend of a friend (or something like that). More importantly, she had a high school senior, and she was very concerned about the upcoming transition. I listened as Rose discussed how her child was not ready for the challenges of college, with only a few months before graduation. Over the weekend, Rose had bought my book *Lost in Transition:Becoming Spiritually Prepared for College* and, like a lot of parents, read it before giving it to their child. After just reading half of the book, she said that it made her even more worried than she was already because of some of the real-life stories I tell in the book. She could see her daughter doing the same thing. Then she said something profound; she stated, "I wish we had been focusing on this stuff years before now." She went on to say that her daughter had grown up in church, but Rose was concerned that her daughter had not learned enough to continue growing in her faith once she left home and ventured out on her own. The truth is, Rose was right. Even one full year is not enough time to focus on the transition if the goal is faith ownership.

Therefore, now that you understand the Ownership Wheel, I want us to look at how to start with your youngest class of teenagers with a transition-focused approach to discipleship. Here are four reasons why this should be an important part of your overall ministry plan.

First, discipleship is best communicated over a consistent, long-range model. They say that an individual does not fully understand something until the 3rd time it is explained. They say that an individual does not fully understand something until the 3rd time it is explained. I hear that an individual does not fully understand something that they are told until the 3rd time they hear it. Get the point? I'd say that, for the average teenager, that number might even be more like five or six, or even twenty times. So the sooner you start, the better off you will be.

Secondly, ownership should always be the end goal to discipleship, and for a teenage-based ministry, graduation and this transition is the end of that journey before students move into a post-high school ministry group. You know how long you have each teen in your ministry. That date is set, unless they leave sooner. Ownership is the goal, and the season for your direct influence usually ends once the tassel is moved.

Third, a transition-focused plan for discipleship is nothing more than teaching the foundational principles of faith and then applying it to the new environment that the student will be moving into. Take another transition for example. If you were preparing a couple for marriage, you would reinforce the Biblical principles of communication, commitment, service, and spiritual growth, and then apply those concepts to the context of marriage. The same goes for the transition after high school. Therefore, if you are working with 8th graders, who are not focused on the college-aged years yet, they can still understand the principles of identity, community and faith ownership.

The fourth reason this is important is because the parents associated with your students need to be trained for what to expect as their child gets older and prepares to leave the nest and be on his own. This takes time. If you begin to meet regularly with the parents when their kids enter the student ministry, it will become a normal occurrence by the time those kids enter the senior year.

## Implementing the Ownership Wheel

I want you to think about what would it look like to create an ownership-focused discipleship plan for the younger classes in your ministry so that when they become seniors, they have already begun the process of preparing for life on their own. One option would be to take the twelve-step Ownership Wheel and split it up into twelve monthly parts. For seventh graders, for example, you would take a topic each month and present it on their level, as you move throughout the year. The next year, you would do it again but this time on an 8th grade level, and so on. That schedule would look something like this:

January: Person of Jesus
February: Identity in Christ
March: Community
April: Loving the Church
May: Understanding Worship
June: Learning Scripture
July: Serving Others
August: Christ-like Worldview
September: Apologetics
October: Christ-like Character
November: Becoming a Christian Leader
December: Owning Your Faith

You could literally use that list each month of each year through the 11th grade as you change the approach and level of understanding as your students grow in age and maturity. As far as content, that would be up to you as to if you found books on those topics, wrote your own lessons, or found established curriculums that deal with each of these topics.

Another option would be to take the twelve topics on the wheel and use them quarterly for your middle school and high school groups. Therefore, the middle school would move through the wheel in twelve quarters, covering each topic in three years. For example, if using my list, the first year would cover The Person of Christ, Identity, Community, and Worship. The second year would include Scripture, The Church, Serving, and Worldview. The last year in the cycle would be a study on Apologetics, Character Development, Leadership, and then Faith Ownership. Then you would have the option to repeat the cycle for the next 3 years or until your students are seniors, depending on if you begin in the 6th or 7th grade for youth ministry. Throughout this process, you should include service opportunities, fellowship gatherings, Scripture memory, and parent meetings to inform them of what you are doing and to help strengthen the partnership you have with them.

In an ideal scenario, students enter their senior year with an understanding of faith and years of experiencing the Ownership Wheel, so that now they only need to understand how to transition their faith to the new setting of college or other post-graduation environments. They will value the church and community and know that the first thing they must do is replace those influences after graduation. They will know who they are in Christ and what they believe in the Word. They will see the world through the eyes of Christ and will know that they are called to love and serve the world around them. They will see themselves as a leader and the light of the world, and will have already begun to develop ownership and be responsible for themselves and their decisions. This is not an overly idealistic vision for your ministry. This is the result of years of effective discipleship with a goal of developing ownership in your students by the time they graduate from your ministry.

## Chapter Five Questions:

How have you seen ownership become the central factor in students who have either struggled in the transition or those who have not?

How could you use the Ownership Wheel to re-structure your discipleship strategy to prepare your students for life after high school?

What topics would you add or change from your personal Ownership Wheel?

What are a few take-away points from this chapter that you feel were most important to you and your ministry?

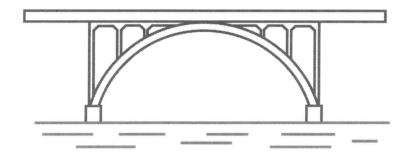

## Chapter Six - The Senior Year Initiative

In the last chapter, I introduced the Ownership Wheel and laid out how it can be used for your students, from your youngest to oldest grades. The main reason you would want to begin this process with your youngest class is to lay a foundation of faith so that when those students reach the senior year, they will be ready for your senior year initiative.

There is one distinct difference in approaching discipleship to high school seniors, as opposed to the younger classes. If you have spent the years, prior to the senior year, equipping your students for faith ownership, then your priority with seniors is to take those faith principles and apply them to the new setting of college or other post graduation environments. I will explain that further when we discuss curriculum.

As you plan to develop a senior year initiative, you are going to want to prepare them adequately, utilize their leadership potential, and send them off well. In this chapter, I will present a model for a senior year initiative plan. Before I share it with you, I want you to understand a few things about it. First, this is an in-depth plan; therefore, you do not have to be the one to lead this plan. I know you are already doing too much, so feel free to delegate the senior year initiative to someone else in your ministry. Secondly, this senior year initiative has room for you to cater it to your needs. You do not have to do it just as I have laid it out. Thirdly, creating a senior year initiative is as easy as making a sandwich. No, that is not a misprint; I did say, "a sandwich." Let me explain.

What makes a good sandwich? Is it the meat? How about the bread? Cheese? Actually, if you are like me, you say "All of the above." A good sandwich is all about what you put in it, and the same applies to a good senior year initiative. So, let's build a sandwich...I mean, let's plan a solid senior year initiative.

## The Bread - Bookending Events

The first part of making a sandwich is finding the right bread. The bread serves as the bookends of a good sandwich, and the same could be said for a senior year initiative. When creating a year-long plan for your seniors, the bread signifies two book-ending events, one at the beginning of the school year and the second at the end, just before graduation. The top piece of bread represents a party at the beginning of the school year to communicate the importance of this last year of high school. This can be a dinner or lunch together where your students talk about the best memories of the past and you then introduce the fact that this senior year is going to be different. You can mention your expectations for the seniors to step up as the leaders of the youth group and that you have some special responsibilities and opportunities for them this year. Your goal is for these students to walk away from this first event with a sense of excitement for the year and feeling honored to be a senior in your student ministry. This is a big deal, so make this first event special. This event will begin to establish a tradition in your ministry that the seniors are set apart, honored, and given the opportunity to serve, lead, and do some things that the younger kids can look forward to. This will all become more clear as we continue to build our sandwich.

*As you plan to develop a senior year initiative, you are going to want to prepare them adequately, utilize their leadership potential, and send them off well.*

The second, bottom piece of bread represents a year-ending, senior recognition event. This one is more common and may already be done at your church. This event, usually held in the weeks or days before graduation, often includes the parents and can include a presentation of the students during a

Sunday morning worship service. I think this is important to wrap up the year-long focus, and like the bottom piece of bread on a sandwich, it holds everything together.

## The Meat - Transition-Focused Content

Now that we have the bread laid out, it is time to put the meat on our sandwich. The meat is like protein for the soul. Without the meat, a sandwich has no substance; even a BLT has the B. The meat of your senior plan represents the content that will guide these students to a healthy, faithful transition out of high school and into the next chapter of life. I suggest you break this up into two parts: fall semester and spring semester.

The first piece of meat, during the fall of the senior year, can be centered around the fundamentals of growing and maturing in Christ. You might look back at the Ownership Wheel and take a few of those categories to go deeper into, than in years past. For example, take the subject of community. This is a very important topic for students heading to college. In the 10th and 11th grades, you may have looked at community by discussing how to love our neighbor and introducing the concept of accountability to the students. During the fall of the senior year, you might look at Acts 1 of the first Christians and how this level of community goes against every natural behavior of our current culture. This would provide a great discussion for free thinking high school seniors.

The second piece of meat represents the content during the second semester of the senior year. This should involve taking all that has been learned in the fall and applying it in the context of college (or other post-graduation destinations). So, take our community example. Again you need to apply the topic of community in the context of college by asking questions such as: 1) How will you replace the influence of this church and ministry once you move away? and 2) Why is finding a Christ-centered community of friends important to continuing to grow in college? Then, throughout the year, you answer the question by giving them steps for how to find a new church, new accountability, a group to worship with and serve along side, friends for fellowship, and a mentor for discipleship and growth. Other examples for the spring might be expectations for college, faith ownership, life management issues such as time and money management, and goal setting.

In the back of this book, I have included some of the transition resources that I have written and how those can help you put some meat on the sandwich of your plan. My book, *Lost in Transition*, was designed to provide a solid semester-long curriculum to help enrich every topic on the Ownership Wheel to a class of high school seniors. The truth is, meat makes the sandwich and is the core ingredient to your overall senior transition plan. Don't skimp on the meat!

## The Toppings - Topping off the Experience

Now that we have the meat for our sandwich, it is time to add the third component: the toppings. Lettuce, tomato, mayo, and spicy mustard can turn a sub into a masterpiece. Likewise, adding a few toppings to an already great transition plan is like the big olive on top.

The purpose of adding toppings to this experience is to find a few opportunities to make the year memorable. As you think of what that can be, ask yourself, "What would they love to do this year that would set them apart as seniors?" This might include leadership roles, a senior mission trip or service project, a senior road trip just for fun, or a senior breakfast, lunch, or dinner once a month.

I feel that this component is often overlooked, and I can understand why. The ministry year is already busy enough without adding more items on a full calendar, but I am convinced that after the experience, you will be glad you planned it. Remember, you do not have to be the one to lead all of this. You can delegate it to volunteers, Sunday School teachers, parents, or others so that this single class focus does not take you over the edge. The important thing is that this year is one that seniors remember, both in content preparation, as well as making memories and developing responsibility.

The senior year should be special. Seniors should be expected to do more, in regards to leadership, and allowed privileges and opportunities that others can only look forward to. When I was in high school, we went to this one camp every summer at the beach. All of the cabins were the same except for one that was set apart and "slightly" nicer. We called it the White House because it was painted white, while the others were blue. By the time I got to the youth group, it was a known tradition that the seniors stayed in the White House with the coolest counselors. I remember looking forward to staying in the White House (I once got to walk in the White House as a sophomore, which in and of itself was special). My senior year, we took pride in staying there and spent hours staying up and talking with our music minister about all the funny things that we did throughout the years on choir tour that he never knew about. We laughed until the early morning hours. It was special. I still remember that week to this day.

More importantly than staying in a senior cabin or getting to go on a special retreat, seniors need to be challenged to lead in your ministry. If you are not giving your seniors leadership roles, you are missing an opportunity to build disciples. This is important for two reasons. First, your seniors are your oldest and (hopefully) most mature students in your ministry. They need to set the example and be given opportunities to shine their light. This might include an upfront role on stage, serving as a middle school Bible study leader, or it might include a behind-the-scenes role of helping plan the activity calendar and set up for events. This is also important because your seniors need to be given leadership roles. They do not need to simply be participants in your ministry for the sixth time. They need to get involved and experience it from the perspective of an emerging adult.

If you are unwilling to make the senior year special, you might not have any seniors in the coming years. As I mentioned in an earlier chapter, many youth ministries lose seniors because these students are tired of the same old song and dance. But, if they know that this year will be different and one they would not want to miss, trust me, they will not miss it. Seniors already feel like they have moved on, yet everything at school and home is still the same. Let church be the one place that understands that about them and realizes that they are older and, therefore, treats them that way. Serve them by appealing to their desire to be different. Make them stand up as leaders and reward them for being active in your ministry for all of these years. Let them be seniors!

## Chapter Six Questions:

Why do you think it is difficult for many youth ministries to develop and execute a full year senior transition strategy and plan?

What is the value of planning two bookend events at the beginning and end of the school for seniors?

What are some of the essential characteristics needed for the content (meat) of the senior initiative to be effective?

How does adding some toppings into the year-long senior plan help the students develop a more well-rounded foundation of preparation for the upcoming transition?

What are a few take-away points from this chapter that you feel were most important to you and your ministry?

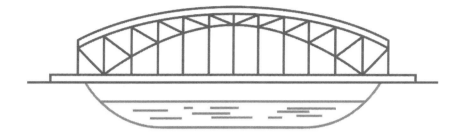

## Chapter 7 - The Follow-Up Plan

About two weeks into my college journey, I saw a sign on the dorm bulletin board advertising a Back-To-School Worship Event at a campus ministry that I had heard of before. At this point, I was still very open to connecting to a ministry on my new campus that would provide me with Christian friends, corporate worship, and opportunities for ongoing mentoring and discipleship. I asked a few of my new friends to go with me, but no one would, so I went on my own. I was nervous and secretly hoping that the event was canceled because I had already become extremely aware that even the slightest association to a college group was identity forming (good or bad). I got to the door of the building and timidly walked in. This would be the first time I had ever gone to a Christian event on my own without anyone expecting me.

I could smell pizza and hear music playing in the next room. I saw other students hanging out in the main room, but I did not recognize any of them. I stood there for what seemed like ten minutes but was probably only about ten seconds, and then I turned around and left. I never went back. I have thought about that night a thousand times since then. What if I had stayed that evening? Would there have been a chance that all of my upcoming faith struggles would have been minimized or possibly non-existent? Who knows? What I do know is that I was the type of guy who could have come right out of high school and been an influential light, shining brightly on my campus, but I did not have that perspective.

What would have been helpful to me at that time would have been to have someone committed to follow-up with me occasionally during that first semester. In a world before social media or even texting, I think someone calling or even sending a letter (remember those?) would have been something that I would have appreciated, especially from a mentor. To have had someone ask me about my search for Christian community might have been the encouragement I needed to step through that door with confidence.

## Three Reasons You Need A Follow-Up Plan

In this chapter, I want to focus on developing a follow-up plan for your students. So, why do you need to have a follow-up plan? Here are three reasons for developing a follow-up plan for students who have recently graduated and moved away from home.

First, you need a follow-up plan because you love people. No matter how well you knew any particular student in high school, you still love them because Jesus loves them. You know that the transition they are going through is hard, and living in a new environment and finding new friends can be scary at first. So, if for no other reason, follow up because you are called to love others.

The second reason to have a follow-up plan is because you still have influence over your former students. When someone is a mentor to us, we always see them in that role, no matter how old we get. Until a student gets involved in a new church or ministry and feels comfortable with new leaders and mentors, you may be the most important mentoring influence in that person's life. Take responsibility of that opportunity and continue to offer leadership and guidance.

The third reason to have a follow-up plan is because students need for you to have one. Even the most well prepared and mature teenager needs someone to check in and provide accountability, especially during this transition. I would even go so far to say that if you fail to develop a follow-up plan for your graduated students then your overall transition effort will be incomplete and unfinished. This is a very important last step in the overall transition process.

So, what does a follow-up plan entail? Is it more than calling or texting them once, mid-way through the fall semester? Does it include a visit or a care-package? To all of those questions, yes, yes, and absolutely yes! There is no true measuring stick for what makes a good follow-up plan. The important thing is that the student feels the following four emotional reactions from it. First, you want them to feel loved. They probably feel alone on an island and feel, at least slightly, homesick; so hearing from you and knowing that you (still) care, will make them feel loved and appreciated. Secondly, you want them to feel cared for. You have been preparing them for this journey for many years, so to check in and make sure that they remember all of the faith principles you taught them will give them a sense that they are cared for. Thirdly, you want them to feel the assurance that if they needed something, you are still available to them. And last but not least, you want them to understand that how they are doing spiritually matters to you and other people that love them. Again, I think that would have been just what I needed during my first few months after starting college.

## A Four Step Follow-Up Model

So, here is how to develop a follow-up plan for your students the semester after they leave your ministry and start college. First, start by telling them, at some point during their senior year, to expect for you to follow up with them the following year. This will not only give you the accountability to do it, but it will also let them know to expect it.

Second, commit to a five finger point of contact. Here is what I mean. Hold up your hand and make a fist. Don't worry if you are in a coffee shop and in public, just hold up your fist. Now, as I name off five ways to make contact, I want you to release a finger from your grip. Ready? Call, Text, Mail, Message, and Visit. Did you do it? Are people staring at you now?

Depending on how many graduates you have, this might take some help, but let's say that you had twenty seniors last year. The first contact is to call, so pick a week in early September, and call four students each day for a week. Give them each a call on their cell phones and ask them how things are going. Ask a few questions about community, grades, social life and maybe something about new friends and their roommate. Depending on your relationship, this call might take a couple minutes or thirty. The important thing is, they know you are there and that you care. Within a week, with just a few minutes each day, you have called all of your 20 former students.

The next contact is to text. I recommend that you give it two or three weeks from when you called, and text them to let them know you are praying for them, and you hope to see them soon when they come home. The third finger (watch where you point that, by the way) stands for mailing. Sometime around mid-terms, you can get some people in your church to make cookies and donate some things to put into a care-package for each of your graduated seniors. You might give them a devotional and include a hand written letter from someone in the church. Send those boxes off to arrive during mid-term exams, and know that each box will speak loudly about how much you and the church love its students.

The fourth contact is to send a message. This can be via email, or over social media, and lets the students know that you look forward to seeing them over the holidays. Remind them about the Sunday morning schedule for college students at your church, and tell them about the breakfast that you will have over the holidays (which is step three of this plan). The fifth form of contact is to plan a visit. This can happen in one of two ways. If you have a few students on a campus within driving distance, drive up to meet them for lunch and catch up. If that is not possible, plan to visit them the day or two after they get home for Thanksgiving or Christmas of their freshman year. Catch up at their home, and invite them to a special time at church where they can fellowship with all of their friends.

If you take this time to do the five finger point of contact during that first semester, you will help your students transition well and help them to stay connected to you and your church. Not only that, this will make the parents VERY happy and thankful.

The third step, as I alluded to a moment ago, is to plan a breakfast during Sunday School over the holidays for all returning college students to make them feel welcome and connected. This is an easy sell to the parents and other church members to plan and prepare. I suggest asking members of your church to make the food so that you can focus on getting the students there. You might consider inviting your current senior class to come, which could serve as one of the traditional "Toppings" of their senior initiative plan. For your current seniors, this would be an opportunity to hear how the transition to college has gone for the older students and provide a time for you to encourage this entire group.

The forth and final step in your needed follow-up plan is to provide weekly discipleship opportunities for students when they are home. This might mean starting a college Sunday School class if you don't have one, with a leader who is called to continue teaching and reaching out to college students. You might already have this. Many churches have a staff person for college ministry, but if you do not, you should find a volunteer to serve in that role. The college students in your church should learn who this person is before they begin this transition, so that when they do come home, it will seem like a natural step to come under that person's leadership. If many of your students live close to home, then you might even consider a weekly college Bible study to continue discipling those students. Someone in the church might open up their home and cook a meal for the college students, which will become a big draw for those looking for opportunities of discipleship and fellowship.

*If you fail to develop a follow-up plan for your graduated students, then your overall transition effort will be incomplete and unfinished.*

After the first semester in college, I give you permission to pull back from your college students and pass the responsibility to someone else so that you can focus on your current group. All I think you, or someone on your team, needs to do is the five contacts, plan a breakfast one Sunday morning during the holiday season, and then set up a college-aged contact for future ministry. This should not take too much of your time away from your regular ministry responsibilities. This is important and will go a long way in helping these students make a healthy transition after high school.

Ministry is a journey, not a sprint. A very wise mentor of mine once told me to always meet a teenager like you will know them for the rest of your life, because that might be the case. That has certainly proven true over and over in my life and ministry. I have close friends today who were in those first years of my ministry. Many of them still see me as a mentor and come to me when they have a question, or a problem, or when they want me to officiate their wedding. Those friends represent some of the most special ministry relationships I have ever had, but none of them would have continued to grow if I had not intentionally stayed in touch with them while in college and then after. Treat your teenage friends like you will know them when they are your age now and older, because you can make an impact in the lives of your students for much longer than just a few years while they are in high school.

## Chapter Seven Questions:

Think about your past follow-up plan, if you've had one, for recent graduates during their first year away from the youth ministry. How was it effective? What was it lacking?

Why is a follow-up plan important to both the students and your ministry? What are the main needs that a good follow-up plan should meet in the life of the student?

Evaluate your current college-aged ministry effort. How are you providing community and discipleship for church members away at college and for local college students who may be living in your area?

What are a few take-away points from this chapter that you feel were most important to you and your ministry?

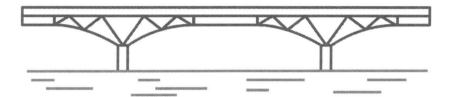

# Chapter 8 - Transition Central

In this book, I have tried to answer two main questions for you in your ministry. First is the "why" question: Why is the transition after high school so challenging? As I have tried to answer that question, my hope is that you already have a better understanding of the struggles that this transition can create. Secondly, is the question of "how": How do you structure your ministry so that your are sending your students out prepared for life after high school? Through the Ownership Wheel, a senior initiative, and follow-up plan, I hope that you already have the beginnings of a vision for how to best reach the goals you have made.

Now, as a final step, I would like to sum all of this up by telling you about something I call Transition Central (TC). Transition Central is a process for how to put all of this into action for your students. TC has four steps and, by reading this book, you have already completed step one.

1. The first step is to read this book. Unless you have skipped to the end and are reading this first, you are already well on your way. After reading this book, you will understand the importance of putting such an emphasis on this transition.

2. Step two is to complete the Vision and Ministry Plan in the back of this book (also available to print out at www.thetransmission.org/resources). This will help you complete your student exit strategy and begin to complete your Ownership Wheel and Senior Plan.

3. The third step is to make you aware of a full range of resources that can help you reach your established goals. To give you an idea of the additional resources that I have available, read the next few pages and then take note as to how I advise using these materials. For more than two decades, I have been focusing my ministry attention on this transition and producing materials to guide students and parents over this gap. I want to share four books with you that will create a foundation of transitional discipleship in your church. This list includes two books to use during the senior year, one for parents of younger children to raise their kids with those transitional challenges in mind, and a devotional for a student's first semester in college. Also, I want you to be aware of an annual online resource that is free to use for the church or individual families called the Senior Summit. Over the years in ministry, I have seen these resources prepare thousands of students and families. My desire is that this book and these

additional resources will help equip the families in your church to prepare teenagers with faith ownership by the time they leave home and begin this transition after high school.

## Transition Resources

*Lost in Transition: Becoming Spiritually Prepared For College.* This book is in its 3rd edition and over the past 10 years has helped thousands of

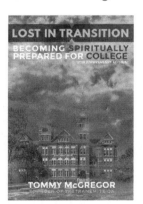

students prepare for the transition to college. Now with a full study guide included in the back of the book, this book could provide you with an 8-12 week senior study during the fall or spring semester of the 12th grade year.

The best way I can describe the structure of *Lost in Transition* is to say that the book has three main goals. First, is to help the student know who they are. The first few chapters focus on identity in Christ and what it means to follow Jesus. This is the foundation of gaining ownership and the most important component to this transition. Secondly, I want students to understand the environment in which they will be transitioning to. Chapter three is called "College Life" and describes the culture of college and how it is different from high school. After helping the student know who they are and where they are going, the third and final goal is to learn how they can remain themselves in that new setting. This is the key to making a healthy transition after high school. As I mentioned in chapter one of this book, transitioning students are leaving the four main influences behind, and they must learn to re-establish those relationships in their new environment. This starts with remaining who they are and understanding what it will take to continue the trajectory of maturity in college.

This book is also helpful to students who may not be going away to college or going to college at all. The setting will be different, but the steps to making a healthy transition remain the same. To learn more about the book, read samples, and download a free teaching guide, go to this link: www.thetransmission.org/books.

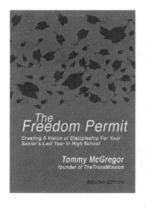

***The Freedom Permit: Creating A Vision of Discipleship For Your Senior's Last Year in High School*** is a book for parents of seniors. This book will help those parents maximize the senior year and prepare their senior for this transition. The book is divided into four sections: Spiritual Development, Life Management, Social Behaviors, and Goal Setting. Each section is presented with questions to ask the senior, Scripture to read, and activities to do together. I teach this book to parents of juniors and seniors each year, and many parents step up to the challenge of discipleship and find this book to be a helpful guide to use throughout that last year of high school.

The name of the book comes from the book's theme. When a teenager turns 16, he gets his first experience with real freedom when he gets his driver's license. But this is not the first time he has been behind the wheel of an automobile. The year before, he has his driver's permit and has to learn how to handle the freedoms of driving, with Mom or Dad in the passenger seat. So, we take that concept to the senior year when the teenager prepares for a larger batch of freedoms. This time he gets a freedom permit, which represents a year to learn how to handle the freedoms of life on his own, hopefully with Mom and Dad still in the passenger seat. To learn more about the book, read samples, and download an introduction video to show parents, go to this link: www.thetransmission.org/books.

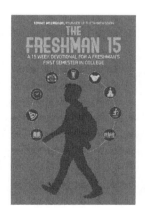

***The Freshman 15*: a 15 week devotional for a freshman's first semester in college** is a great addition to your overall transition plan. This book will give your students a 15-week daily devotional that will touch on many of the issues and challenges a student will face that first semester in college. Each week of that first semester, the reader will explore one of fifteen faith principles that will lead him or her to discover overall health and well-being during this very important life transition. This book is organized so that every week, the student will grow spiritually, memorize Scripture, answer questions, and be challenged based on the weekly theme. To learn more about the book and download the introduction and first five weeks of content, go to www.thefreshman15book.com.

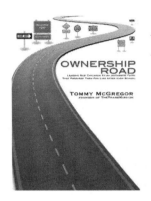

***Ownership Road: Leading Our Children To An Authentic Faith That Prepares Them For Life After High School*** is a book for parents of younger children, approximate ages 5-15. This could be a good book study for the parents of your middle school students or even younger. This book calls the parent to the Biblical role of the CDO (Chief Discipling Officer); then it walks the parent through how to raise young kids with the post-high school challenges in mind. As parents learn how to disciple, they will understand the path from followship to ownership. Followship is learning what it truly means to follow Jesus, and ownership is taking responsibility of that relationship. Just like I challenged you in chapter four of *Bridging The Gap*, in *Ownership Road* I challenge parents to lead their children to a place of faith ownership by high school graduation. As a youth ministry leader, I want to encourage you to see the potential of developing a true discipling partnership with your students' parents as you work to reach the same goal of ownership by graduation.

Also available is a personal study guide called the *Ownership RoadMap, which is* for parents to use in a small group setting. *Ownership Road* is a twelve chapter book and is ideal for a 10-12 week small group study. To learn more about the book and read samples, go to this link: www.thetransmission.org/books.

The Senior Summit is an annual online video course that I use to help students dive deeper into the process of making a healthy transition to college. Each year I interview people on the front lines of this transition, from authors and campus ministry leaders, to experts in various fields related to this transition. This series will help high school seniors learn how to better prepare for the challenges associated with the transition from high school to college. The Senior Summit usually releases in the mid to late fall each year and you can learn more about how to use this in your overall senior initiative by going to www.thetransmission.org/summit.

To help you fully see how these resources work in relationship to your vision plan, look at the chart on the next page. You will see these books and video series in a particular order, beginning with preparing parents of younger

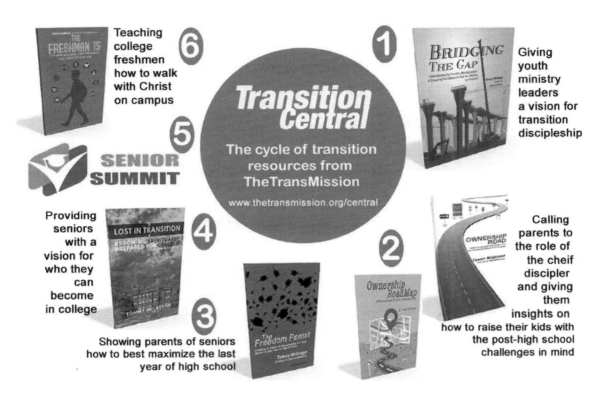

**Transition Central**

The cycle of transition resources from TheTransMission

www.thetransmission.org/central

6 — Teaching college freshmen how to walk with Christ on campus

1 — Giving youth ministry leaders a vision for transition discipleship

5 — SENIOR SUMMIT

2 — Calling parents to the role of the cheif discipler and giving them insights on how to raise their kids with the post-high school challenges in mind

4 — Providing seniors with a vision for who they can become in college

3 — Showing parents of seniors how to best maximize the last year of high school

children, all the way to guiding your freshmen in college. For group discounts and video intros on these book studies, go to www.thetransmission.org/central.

Using any of these resources will help your students prepare for this transition, but let me give you some examples of how you can use these books, and other content shared in this book, collectively in your ministry. As you look at your ministry with a wide lens, you are going to want to start early to begin leading your students to a place of ownership by graduation. This will require a team approach, along with the children's ministry leaders of your church, to do the job well. I recommend beginning with parents of pre-teens by having parents do a study of *Ownership Road*. This will help parents to start thinking in the right ways and cast your vision before their children get into middle school.

Secondly, I would implement the Ownership Wheel in the seventh grade and have it taught through the eleventh grade. Each spring, I would have a meeting with the parents of your juniors and talk to them about the senior year initiative. At that meeting, I would pass out copies of *The Freedom Permit* and summarize how to use the book.

Beginning each fall, I would have the first of two senior events to share a vision with your seniors that includes your intentions to make the year a special one, as well as your expectation that they will step into leadership roles in the student ministry this year. I would spend some time recapping the Ownership Wheel and applying those principles to the setting of life after high school. I would then begin teaching *Lost in Transition,* using the chapter-by-chapter study guide and additional articles in the back to make that a 12-week study. Along with the book, I would use the Senior Summit series videos intermittently or after the book study. I would consider a senior spring break trip &/or service project, and a senior recognition service just before graduation. At that time, I would give each senior a copy of *The Freshman 15* and share more about my follow-up plan to keep in touch with them during the fall of the next year.

With this action plan, I would feel good about reaching my goal of preparing students for ownership by the time they graduate. This plan would include a long-term vision (*Ownership Road*, Ownership Wheel), involve parents (*Ownership Road*, *The Freedom Permit*), incorporate a strong senior year initiative (Ownership Wheel, *Lost in Transition*), and a solid follow-up plan (5 finger contact, *The Freshman 15*).

4. The forth and final step of Transition Central is to consider staying in touch with me so that I can hear how your ministry is going and answer any questions that you might have. It is a highlight for me in ministry when I can get to know student ministry leaders and hear how they are leading teenagers to Jesus. I am available for a conversation and I hope you will reach back out to set something up soon. The easiest way to set up a time for us to talk is to go to www.calendly.com/thetransmission and find a time that your and I are available.

Now that you have made it through this book, I ask that you take some time to process this material. To help you do this, I have included a vision and outline plan on the following nine pages (also available to print at www.thetransmission.org/resources).

## Bridging The Gap
## Transition Vision Plan

These last few pages are intended to allow you space to create your transition vision plan. All of the previous questions in this workbook should have helped you communicate some of the questions and ideas that you have about your potential transition plan. Use your answers to those questions to develop a plan that caters to your needs regarding your students and ministry.

In a few sentences, describe what your end goal for a transition plan would be. What do you hope your students will learn and be prepared for as they transition out of high school and into the next chapter of life?

Use your answer to the question on the previous page to help you generate a mission statement for your senior transition plan.

Now, take your mission statement and the answer to the first question in the section and develop your Student Exit Strategy Statement. Note that your transition mission statement and your student exit strategy might seem similar in purpose, but they are different in how they serve your planning. While the mission statement sets an overall purpose to your plan (including why you have a plan and how you will prepare your students), the exit strategy describes the place of maturity that you hope your students will reach when they graduate from your student ministry.

# Bridging The Gap
# Transition Outline Plan

PART ONE: The Senior Study Plan

Looking back at the concept of making a sandwich, fill in the blanks in this outline with specific ideas for each of the three parts of the senior plan.

### Bread: Bookending Events

Fall Senior Event Ideas:

Spring Senior Event Ideas:

**Meat: Senior Transition Content**

Fall Semester Content and Curriculum Ideas:

Spring Semester Content and Curriculum Ideas:

## **Toppings: Extra Opportunities for Seniors**

Senior Leadership Ideas:

Senior Service Ideas:

Senior Activity Ideas:

PART TWO: The Non-Senior Study Plan

Looking back at your notes and answers from session eight, fill in the blanks in this outline with specific ideas for how to structure a transition plan for your other classes of students.


Thinking through the 12 points on the Ownership Wheel and any others that you added to the question in chapter 6, create a full list of topics to teach students prior to the senior class study.

Now, organize those topics for each grade on a separate notepad/whiteboard by using a structure like this:

Grade _____
Teaching Theme:

This will help these students reach the exit strategy goal in this way:
Week 1 / Quarter 1:
Week 2 / Quarter 2:
Week 3 / Quarter 3:
Week 4 / Quarter 4:
(Break into specific weeks or quarters with topics, themes, verses, questions)


PART THREE: The Follow-Up Plan

Think through your notes and answers from the session on following up and then fill in the blanks below to develop your plan.


**Step One: The Commitment**
The best time for me to announce to seniors that I will be following up with them the next fall is:

**Step Two: The Five Finger Point of Contact**
Below is a target date for you (&/or someone in your ministry) to do each of the 5 points of contact:

Call:

Text:

Mail:

Message:

Visit:

**Step Three: College Breakfast**

Target Date:

Location:

Person in Charge of Breakfast:

Details:

**Step Four: College Ministry Component**

The best person to head up a college ministry for our students is:


Details on time/location, curriculum, etc:


Additional Notes:

## About The Author:

Tommy McGregor is an author, speaker and the founder of TheTransMission, a ministry devoted to guiding high school seniors to a healthy spiritual transition to college. He is the author of seven books, as well as numerous published articles, e-books, video courses, and other transition related resources.

Tommy has spent over two decades working with high school and college students in church and para-church ministry, and is passionate about helping others develop a sense for who God has created them to be. He lives in Montgomery, Alabama with his wife & their two boys.

## Contact:

Ministry Website: www.thetransmission.org
Blog: www.tommymcgregor.com
Email: tommy@thetransmission.org
Facebook: www.facebook.com/TransMissionOrg
Twitter: @tommymcgregor